Susanna Wesley

WOMEN OF FAITH SERIES

Amy Carmichael
Corrie ten Boom
Florence Nightingale
Gladys Aylward
Isobel Kuhn

Joni
Madame Guyon
Mary Slessor
Susanna Wesley

MEN OF FAITH SERIES

Andrew Murray
Borden of Yale
Brother Andrew
C. S. Lewis
Charles Colson
Charles Finney
Charles Spurgeon
D. L. Moody
E. M. Bounds
Eric Liddell
George Muller
Hudson Taylor
Jim Elliot

John Calvin
John Hyde
John Newton
John Paton
John Wesley
Jonathan Goforth
Luis Palau
Martin Luther
Oswald Chambers
Samuel Morris
William Booth
William Carey

WOMEN AND MEN OF FAITH

John and Betty Stam
Francis and Edith Schaeffer

OTHER BIOGRAPHIES FROM BETHANY HOUSE

Autobiography of Charles Finney
George MacDonald: Scotland's Beloved Storyteller
Hannah Whitall Smith
Help Me Remember, Help Me Forget (Robert Sadler)
Janette Oke: A Heart for the Prairie
Miracle in the Mirror (Nita Edwards)
Of Whom the World Was Not Worthy (Jakob Kovac family)

Susanna Wesley

Kathy McReynolds

BETHANY HOUSE PUBLISHERS
MINNEAPOLIS, MINNESOTA 55438

Susanna Wesley
Copyright © 1998
Katherine McReynolds

The language in this book has been updated for the modern reader.

Cover by Dan Thornberg,
Bethany House Publishers staff artist.

Published by Bethany House Publishers
A Ministry of Bethany Fellowship International
11400 Hampshire Avenue South
Minneapolis, Minnesota 55438
www.bethanyhouse.com

Printed in the United States of America by
Bethany Press International
Minneapolis, Minnesota 55438

ISBN 7–7642–2003–9

KATHY McREYNOLDS is a graduate of Biola Univeristy and Talbot School of Theology (M.A.). She served as an adjunct instructor and team teacher at both schools. She has coauthored several books and contributed to several collections. She lives in California with her husband and children.

Contents

Introduction

The apostle Paul tells us that God "determined the times set for [humankind] and the exact places where they should live. God did this so that [humankind] would seek him and perhaps reach out for him and find him, though he is not far from each one of us" (Acts 17:26–27).

To reach out to God and find him is exactly what Susanna Wesley did. Her very difficult circumstances caused her to look beyond herself to him who gives eternal strength. The exact time and place of Susanna's existence, determined by God himself, moved her to his throne of grace.

Susanna Wesley married a man who was constantly kicking against the goads. She became the mother of nineteen children, lived in utter poverty, and experienced a multitude of griefs and hardships during her lifetime.

But the strength and comfort she found in God's everlasting arms carried her through the troubled seasons in her life. And, when it was all said and done, she passed on an extraordinarily rich spiritual heritage to her children. She taught them formally and by example to love and honor God. She gave them an extensive classroom education and, at the same time, showed them the value of reaching out to those in need. The children watched their mother turn her worst enemies into friends of God.

Susanna Wesley had an especially strong impact on her two famous sons, John and Charles Wesley. Throughout their ministry careers, they repeatedly turned to their mother for advice concerning spiritual matters.

In fact, the revival that took place in England and America as a result of John's and Charles' preaching ministry was to a large extent fueled by their mother's teachings.

Many of Susanna's teachings have been preserved in her written manuals and in her letters to her children. Because of this, we have the awesome privilege of becoming intimately acquainted with her.

It is our prayer that you will learn from this woman the value of a steadfast, undaunted faith in God.

1

Susanna's Early Years

As friends and family gathered together to witness the christening of another Annesley child, a friend asked, "How many children has Doctor Annesley?" Someone replied, "I believe it is two dozen, or a quarter of a hundred."[1]

As it turned out, the latter was correct. Susanna Annesley, born in London on January 20, 1669, was the twenty-fifth and final child to enter into the Annesley household.

There is only sketchy information available about Susanna's older brothers and sisters. Most of this centers on Samuel Annesley, Susanna's eldest brother. Through her later years, Susanna kept in close communication with him.

As a young man, Samuel left his home in England and went to India where he founded a lucrative business. The relationship between Samuel and Susanna became strained when his many promises to her of financial blessing went unfulfilled. At one point he boarded a ship bound for England, but he never made it to his destination. Whatever became of Samuel is still shrouded in mystery. He was never seen or heard from again. He

---

[1]John Kirk, *The Mother of the Wesley's: A Biography* (London: Jarrold and Sons, 1868), 23.

either accidentally fell overboard or was robbed, mur-
dered, and purposely cast into the sea.

Besides Samuel and Susanna, we have record of only
five other Annesley children who lived to maturity. Many
of them may have died early in life. If this is the case,
Susanna may not have even known most of her siblings.

No matter how long any of the Annesley children
lived, they unquestionably knew they were loved and
cherished not only by their parents but also by their God.
The Annesleys were deeply devout and wholeheartedly
committed to raising their children to fear the Lord.

Unfortunately, there is very little known about
Susanna's mother—not even her name. However, every
indication seems to point to the fact that she was no
ordinary woman. John Kirk commented,

> The few dim intimations concerning her which have
> turned up in the course of our researches, impress us
> with the idea that she was a woman of superior under-
> standing, and earnest and consistent piety. She was
> deeply loved by her husband, who cherished a passion-
> ate desire to be buried in her grave. She spared no labor
> in endeavoring to promote the religious welfare of her
> numerous children.[2]

Susanna's father, Samuel Annesley, who loved his
wife so deeply, also expressed a similar passion for his
God. He was zealous for the Lord and lived in unre-
strained obedience to his commands.

Annesley was also well known for his charismatic per-
sonality. He was outgoing, friendly, well-educated, and
spiritually gifted. His ultimate purpose was to educate
people in the ways of the Lord.

Samuel's parents, devout Puritans, ignited the spiritual flame early in their son's life. Samuel himself stated

---

[2]Ibid., 20.

he could not remember a time when he did not know the Lord.

At the tender age of five, he began reading twenty chapters of the Bible a day. Throughout his formative years, he developed holy exercises that prepared him for his future career in church ministry.

Early in his teen years, Samuel entered Oxford University. He graduated in 1644 and became a pastor of a church in the county of Kent. Deeply distressed by the ungodly behavior of the people, he determined to do something about it.

Despite threats on his life, Samuel vowed to stay with them until God, through his ministry, had purified them. His perseverance paid off, and soon he witnessed in the people evidence of the grace of God. The Reverend Annesley then moved to London.

This move proved to be one of the greatest challenges in Samuel's life. He soon found himself smack in the middle of England's bloody civil war. On the one hand, England's Royalist army was fighting for King Charles I and the Church of England. The Parliamentarians, on the other hand, were fighting for the Puritans, those who had separated themselves from the Church of England. Oliver Cromwell and the Parliamentarians were the victors, and England experienced a short time of peace.

A few years later the Royalist army and King Charles II regained power. In 1662 Parliament passed a bill known as the Act of Uniformity, ordering all ministers to conform to the practices and beliefs of the Church of England.

Two thousand ministers refused to conform. In what became known as the Great Ejection, these men were strictly forbidden to practice their Puritan faith. Samuel Annesley was among those who protested against the Church of England. As a result, he was immediately thrust from his clerical position.

This banishment undoubtedly brought a great deal of grief and suffering to Samuel and his family, for he was a well paid and highly respected minister. And because of his immense popularity, the Royalists watched him closely.

Constantly heckled and harassed by the authorities, Annesley never lost his determination to serve the Lord according to his Puritan beliefs.

After ten years, King Charles II allowed the Puritans some religious freedom. Wasting no time, Samuel Annesley launched a new ministry. First, he moved his family to Spital Yard, a small, well-to-do neighborhood in London. Then he leased a house in the London district known as Little Saint Helen's, Bishopsgate Street. Almost immediately Reverend Annesley had a thriving, growing congregation. John Kirk said of him:

> Need we wonder that the ministry of such a man was greatly honored by God? Living in the unclouded light of the Divine countenance, and holding unbroken communion with Heaven, his doctrine dropped as the rain, his speech distilled as the dew; "as the small rain upon the tender herb, and as the showers upon the grass." He had great success. Many called him father, as the instrument of their conversion; and many called him comforter.[3]

Samuel Annesley enjoyed above any other religious duty his ministry to the poor, the fatherless, and the widow. The needy and the orphan considered him their refuge from the storms of life. The compassion of Christ poured from him and lifted the countenance of even the most destitute.

Young Susanna was deeply affected by her parents' godly example. She herself said that she was "early ini-

---

[3]Ibid., 16.

tiated and instructed in the first principles of the Christian religion; and had a good example in parents, and in several of the family."[4]

The Annesleys "spared no labor" in making certain that their children witnessed the Christian faith in action. Because of their uncompromising example and their untiring efforts, Susanna wholeheartedly embraced the beliefs of her parents.

However, as Susanna matured, her spirit became unsettled. Though she still accepted her parents' teachings, she became unabashedly curious about many other religious matters. The theological controversies surrounding the Church of England were of particular interest to her.

But it wasn't only religious topics that tickled Susanna's curiosity. She was fascinated with many branches of knowledge. Like her father, she pursued with intensity and determination the things that piqued her interest.

Susanna's parents supported her efforts and encouraged her studies. They took great pains to equip their youngest daughter with a thorough knowledge of the Bible and to provide her with a well-rounded education.

Whether she attended a school or learned at home from her mother is not known. However, since it was not common in those days for girls to receive a formal education, the latter is more likely.

Susanna was endowed with extraordinary mental abilities. She approached every subject with the utmost enthusiasm. Her insatiable hunger for understanding and unquenchable thirst for knowledge drove her to pursue her studies with a vengeance. John Kirk observed:

> Her strong and penetrating mind, perhaps a little too
> self-confident in these early years, feared no difficulty.
> In search of truth, she looked the most formidable objections full in the face. Her attention once aroused to

---

[4]Ibid., 39.

the consideration of a subject, all its perplexities must be canvassed, and honest conclusions attained on the sole ground of its own merits.[5]

Susanna chose to consider abstract and complex subjects. She diligently studied logic, metaphysics, philosophy, and theology. While she did not learn Latin or Greek, she was well versed in French and had a thorough knowledge of English grammar.

It is only when we realize it was highly unusual in Susanna's day for a girl to be knowledgeable in such disciplines that we can truly appreciate her academic achievements.

Young girls, if they were educated at all, were usually trained strictly in domestic duties. But Susanna was blessed with parents who went above and beyond cultural norms. Realizing that Susanna was no ordinary child, they determined to nurture her exceptional intellectual abilities.

Given her religious and academic background, it was only natural that the future Mrs. Wesley would develop a keen understanding of the deep theological controversies surrounding the Church of England in her day.

Susanna was interested in these matters primarily because her father was in the thick of them. Through him, she had firsthand knowledge of the problems. This constant exposure only increased her desire to gain further insight.

Therefore, with the relentless fury that so characterized her, Susanna studied the sticky issues from every possible angle. "Before she was thirteen years of age, she examined without restraint the whole controversy between the Established Church and the Dissenters."[6]

---

[5]Ibid., 29.
[6]Adam Clarke, *Memoirs of the Wesley Family* (New York: Lane and Tippett, 1848), 319.

Having been raised in a Puritan home, she was already thoroughly acquainted with Puritan beliefs and practices. She knew well what her father stood for and what he had sacrificed for his beliefs.

She was also given plenty of opportunities to hear the arguments against the Established Church. Many Dissenters, including John Owen, the "Prince of the Puritans," and Samuel Wesley, visited the Annesley home and debated the issues.

In Susanna's presence, these men openly discussed their differences with the Church of England. Susanna listened attentively while these highly articulate churchmen aired their thoughts and opinions.

Eventually, being overtaken by her unquenchable curiosity, Susanna was compelled to ask some penetrating questions. Soon she became even more bold and "plunged into the talks, and even though she was still a girl, her opinions were attentively heard."[7]

Dr. Annesley was not surprised by his youngest daughter's actions. The other Dissenters, however, were not only shocked by Susanna's knowledge of the subject but were puzzled by her interest in these matters.

---

[7]Ingvar Haddal, *John Wesley: A Biography* (New York: Abingdon Press, 1961), 11.

2

On This Rock I Will Stand

Why would a girl not more than thirteen years of age be concerned about the controversies surrounding the Church of England? Why would she fill her head with theological disputes when she could be learning how to manage the home?

Reform is never easy, but sometimes it is necessary in order to bring about needed change. This was certainly the case for the Church of England in the fifteenth and sixteenth centuries. While the Reformation movement of this time made great strides in bringing about positive change, it was by no means complete by the end of the sixteenth century.

The religious reforms that did take place can be broken down into two broad phases: the Church of England's break with the Roman Catholic Church; and the Puritans' and Separatists' ultimate break with the Church of England.

It was for selfish reasons that King Henry VIII (1509–1547) of England decided to break free from the Pope and the Roman Catholic Church. Henry was married to the lovely Princess Catherine of Aragon, the widow of his older brother Arthur.

Henry and Catherine produced one daughter, Mary, who later became ruler in England. When it was apparent they were not going to produce a son to take his place on the throne, Henry sought a divorce.

When the Pope refused to grant him a divorce, King Henry turned to the English clergy and to Parliament. Through a series of tangled and complex events, Henry persuaded the English clergy to accept him as the head of the Church of England.

The English clergy then granted King Henry a divorce, freeing him to marry the flame of his heart, Anne Boleyn. From this union came yet another daughter, Elizabeth.

Not long after this, the flame in Henry's heart for Anne began to flicker. He divorced her and shortly thereafter married Jane Seymour. She was finally able to give him the true desire of his heart: a son. The king named his one and only son Edward.

Henry VIII accomplished many governmental and religious reforms during his reign. Among them was his successful effort to put an end to papal control and monacistism in England. But it was his son, King Edward VI (1547–1553), who initiated some of the most influential reform measures.

Under Edward's reign, the Church of England went through numerous theological changes. For example, church services were given in English instead of Latin; the Communion cup was for the first time offered to the laity; and the priests were allowed to marry.

When Mary Tudor (1553–1558), daughter of Henry VIII and Catherine of Aragon, came to power, she vigorously opposed the changes and repealed many of the Protestant reform doctrines.

In her zeal to restore Catholicism, Queen Mary ordered the execution of many church leaders, including the influential Archbishop of Canterbury, Thomas Cranmer.

When Elizabeth (1558–1603), daughter of Henry VIII

and Anne Boleyn, took the throne, she overthrew many of the pro-Catholic actions set in motion by Queen Mary, and showed some support for Protestantism. Her own reform began by replacing some Catholic leaders with Protestants.

But she compromised in the matter of church doctrine by restoring both the Articles, which were of the Catholic tradition, and the Prayer Book, the work of Cranmer, a Protestant reformer.

It was during Queen Elizabeth's long reign that the second phase of the religious Reformation began. It started with a group known as the "Elizabethan Puritans," who quickly became a force to be reckoned with in England.

Because of the efforts of King Henry VIII, the Church of England was free from total papal power. But these first Puritans believed there were still too many "rags of popery" within its walls.

Consequently, the Puritans sought to make changes within the church. First and foremost, they wanted to reform the church service. According to church historian Earle Cairns,

> Up until 1570 their main objections were directed against the continued use, in the liturgy of the church, of ritual and vestments that seemed popish to them. They opposed the use of saints' day, clerical absolution, the sign of the Cross, the custom of having godparents in baptism, kneeling for Communion, and the use of the surplice by the minister.[2]

Two more Puritan groups, known as the Presbyterian and Independent Congregational Puritans, began to take shape during this time. These groups were opposed to the

---

[1]Earle Cairns, *Christianity Through the Centuries* (Grand Rapids: Zondervan Publishing, 1981), 335.

Church of England's form of government.

The Presbyterian and Independent Congregational Puritans questioned the validity of the use of bishops. Besides being too reminiscent of Catholic tradition, they did not believe that this model was biblical. According to these groups, church leadership should consist of elders and synods.

Queen Elizabeth did not take too kindly to these Puritan activists. So, in 1593 she took action against them. She ordered that all Puritans must attend the Anglican Church. If they did not comply, they would be put in prison.

It is important to point out, however, that these Puritan groups worked within the Church of England in order to bring about reform. Their overall objective was not to split from the Mother Church but to "purify" it from dead ritual and from extrabiblical practices.

However, in 1567 there arose a more radical group of Puritans known as the Separatists. This group was not interested in making any changes in the Church of England. Rather, their chief objective was to establish their own independence.

In fact, the primary difference between the Separatists and the previously discussed Puritan groups was "the idea of the church covenant by which they bound themselves in loyalty to Christ and one another apart from a state church."[2]

The Separatists held that believers were to bind themselves to Christ and to one another on a voluntary basis and that no congregation was to have authority over the other.[4]

In 1658 the Separatists, along with some Congrega-

---

[2]Ibid., 337.
[3]Ibid., 337.

tional Puritans, developed a creed stating the core of their beliefs:

> The Lord Jesus calleth out of the World unto Communion with himself those that are given unto him by his father. . . . To each of these churches thus gathered, according to his mind declared in his Word, he hath given all that Power and Authority, which is in any way needful for their carrying on that Order in Worship and Discipline, which he hath instituted for them to observe with Commands and Rules, for the due and right exerting of that Power.[4]

During the reigns of James I (1603–1625) and Charles I (1625–1649), the various Puritan groups further entangled themselves in the web of church and government politics.

Because the kings, the Puritans, and the Anglicans each had their own ideas about the way the church should run, there was constant friction between them.

Under the reign of Charles I, the unrest culminated in civil war. Parliament and the Puritans were victorious and, for a time, Puritanistic ideals permeated both the church and the government.

However, the English people began to loathe the Puritan way of life and, in 1660, called Charles II to the throne. He restored the Episcopal model of church government to the Church of England and gave powerful positions to Anglican ministers.[5]

King Charles II also passed the Act of Uniformity, which forbade the Puritans to practice their beliefs. Two thousand Puritan ministers were ejected from their clerical positions. From this time forward, Puritans in England became known as nonconformists or Dissenters.

---

[4]An excerpt from the Savoy Declaration of Faith and Order, 1658.
[5]Cairns, 341.

In the previous chapter, we noted that Samuel Annesley, Susanna Wesley's father, was among those who were cast out of their church positions. This brief history of the controversy between the Church of England and the Puritans shows just how complex the problems were.

But this history does not explain Susanna's interest in the controversy. Why did these problems so capture her attention? Why wasn't she like the other girls her age who were concerned only with domestic duties?

The explanation can be none other than that "in this, as in many other respects, Susanna Wesley was an exception to the general rule."[6] For one thing, she was educated far beyond many girls her own age. Therefore, her world naturally extended beyond the borders of her home.

Also, because Susanna's father was a leading Dissenter, she was privy to many of the historical and theological problems surrounding the Church of England of which other girls were not aware.

But, most importantly, Susanna Annesley had to get involved in the controversy simply because of who she was. Her passionate nature would not allow her to do otherwise.

Susanna was indeed different. And the path of existence God chose for her was also different, destined to be full of many unusual twists and turns.

The first unique turn in Susanna's life came at this point. After rigorously examining the Dissenter's complaints against the Church of England and their proposed principles for reform, Susanna did the unthinkable. She forsook her Puritan faith.

In a letter to one of her children several years later, Susanna wrote about her decision:

And because I was educated among the Dissenters,

---

[6]Kirk, 32.

and there was something remarkable in my leaving them at so early an age, not being fully thirteen, I had drawn up an account of the whole transaction, under which I had included the main of the controversy between them and the Established Church, as far as it had come to my knowledge.[7]

Shortly before she turned thirteen years of age, the future Mrs. Susanna Wesley decided to become a full-fledged member of the Church of England. Her thorough examination of the "controversy between them" led her to believe that the Established Church was right.

Unfortunately, we will never know exactly what she concluded about the controversies because the account she drew up about the matter was destroyed in a fire at the Epworth parsonage.

Nevertheless, it is a well-established fact that Susanna took her stand upon the solid rock of the Church of England and faithfully served the Lord as a member of that church for the rest of her life.

She took that stand alone, for her parents and her siblings remained Dissenters. A few previous biographers have stated that Susanna's decision to leave her Puritan faith caused a great rift between her and her father. However, there is no hard evidence to support this assumption.

In fact, her later writings seem to indicate that she remained close to her father all of her life. When he became ill toward the end of his life, Susanna vigorously prayed for him. After he died, she was "fully persuaded that her father was with her as if she had seen him with her bodily eyes."

Though Susanna's decision was a radical one, it was based on solid inquiry and reflection. For this reason, her father could have had nothing but respect for her. Being

---

[7]Kirk, 32.

a deep thinker and one who made radical decisions himself, he undoubtedly understood her.

It must be remembered that radical thoughts and ideas were nothing new to Susanna. She was raised by a father who was thought to be a radical. And she was raised with Puritan beliefs, which were also considered radical by many in England.

To stand against the tide and to hold to an unpopular view were consistent not only with Susanna's nature but also with her era. Like the fifteenth and the sixteenth centuries, the seventeenth century, in which Susanna lived, was marked by reform and radicalism.

For instance, in the seventeenth century, the king of England and the Established Church had to contend not only with the radical actions of the Puritans but also with the Lutherans and the Calvinists.

Lutheranism and Calvinism did not strike Susanna's interests right away. However, there were some radical reform ideas floating around England at that time which did grab Susanna's attention. These played an extremely important role in her life.

Like Calvinism, these radical ideas originated in Switzerland. Religion flourished in Switzerland because it was the freest country in Europe at that time. Each district was run by a local government and was allowed to choose which form of religion it would follow.

The northern districts primarily adhered to Zwingli's reformed theology, while the southern districts followed Calvin. As these Reformation movements were gaining momentum in Switzerland and in other parts of Europe, the radicals of the Reformation began to emerge.[8]

The Socinians were one of these radical groups. While Socinianism had its roots in Italy, its doctrinal views can be traced back to Switzerland. Lelio Sozzini (1525–1562),

---

[8]Cairns, 301–308.

who became known as Socinus, was a close associate of John Calvin and Philip Melanchthon (colleague of Martin Luther).

For most of his career, Sozzini held to Reformed theology. Eventually, however, he was introduced to anti-Trinitarianism by Michael Servetus of Geneva. His orthodox beliefs began to waver at this point but he continued to hold on to orthodoxy just enough to keep him out of trouble.

Unlike his uncle, Fausto Sozzini (1539–1604) cut all ties to Reformed theology and became a true anti-Trinitarian. In 1579 Fausto moved to Poland and gathered around him a huge following. Before his death in 1604, he gave his followers the Racovian Catechism, which outlined their doctrinal beliefs.

According to Socinus, "Christ is to be worshiped as a man who obtained divinity by his superior life. His death was simply an example of the obedience that God desires from His followers."[9]

Along with his denial of the Trinity and the deity of Christ, Socinus did not hold to the biblical doctrine of original sin or predestination. Socinianism spread from Poland to Holland and then to England.

By Susanna's day, Socinianism was well-established in England. Unfortunately, young Susanna's investigation into the Church of England controversies was not enough to satisfy her ever-increasing intellectual hunger.

So she embarked on an intellectual journey which led her straight to the writings of some famous English Socinists.

[9]Cairns, 308.

3

Samuel and Susanna Wesley

Like Susanna, Samuel Wesley came from a long family history of nonconformists. His grandfather Bartholomew Wesley, born at the end of the sixteenth century, was a devout Puritan. He was educated at Oxford, where he studied medicine and divinity.

Upon graduation, he moved to Dorsetshire and became the vicar of Charmouth and Catherston, which were two small neighborhoods in that county. Bartholomew was honest and direct in his preaching. Though he was respected by his flock, his fiery sermons often hindered his popularity.[1]

Bartholomew entered into the ministry at a time when the Church of England and the nonconformists (Puritans) were in the heat of controversy. Unfortunately, he became an early casualty of these ecclesiastical battles by being thrust from his clerical position.

From this time forward, Rev. Bartholomew Wesley preached only in the shadows and made his living from the practice of medicine. Distraught over the untimely death of his beloved son, John Wesley (not to be confused with John Wesley, son of Susanna and Samuel), this

---

[1]Kirk, 44.

great man was brought to an early grave.

John Wesley, to the day of his death, followed closely in the footsteps of his father and became a powerful preacher of nonconformity. While at Oxford, John became known for his piety and intellect. He so distinguished himself among his peers that he even drew the attention of John Owen, the renowned Prince of the Puritans.

After graduation, Wesley returned to his home in Dorsetshire and began to preach in some of the surrounding towns. In 1658 he took a position at Winterbourn Whitchurch. He then married a daughter of the honorable John White, who was a member of the committee which produced the Westminster Confession of Faith.[2]

Like Susanna's father, Samuel Annesley, John Wesley became a victim of the Great Ejection of 1662. Consequently, he too was driven from his church position. Fleeing from town to town, John dodged the authorities and preached whenever and wherever he could.

In November 1662, Samuel Wesley was born. Like Susanna, Samuel had numerous siblings, many of whom were born before their father was banished. However, besides Samuel, there is record of only three of Wesley's other children: Timothy, Elizabeth, and Matthew.

Despite great trials and suffering, Wesley continued to preach the gospel in secret. At one point, he contemplated moving his family to Maryland but finally decided to suffer for Christ's sake in his homeland.

"Notwithstanding all his prudence in managing his meetings, he was often disturbed; several times apprehended; and four times cast into prison."[3] The fourth imprisonment proved to be too much for him. At age forty-

---

[2]The Westminster Confession of Faith (1646), a document developed by 151 English Puritans and eight Scottish Presbyterians (Westminster Assembly), became the rule of faith for Presbyterianism in the English-speaking world.
[3]Kirk, 47.

two, he was overcome with illness and died.

Consequently, Samuel Wesley, who was attending grammar school at the time of his father's death, was, at such a tender age, deprived of the strong guiding hand of his father. His mother, however, who was poor and now a widow, did the best she could to provide for young Samuel.

Some dissenting friends took Samuel under their wings and sent him to one of their academies in London. When promises for paid tuition fell through at this school, Wesley was sent to the Stepney academy. From there he left to attend the academy at Newington Green.

During the four years Wesley spent at the various dissenting academies, he studied the classics, and also proved himself to be quite gifted in poetry. In the process, he was also exposed to many brilliant Dissenters who harbored strong feelings against the Church of England.

Wesley, in turn, became a strong advocate for the dissenting cause. But, along the way, something started to change in Wesley and he began to doubt his convictions. According to Kirk:

> There was an entire lack of everything like deep experimental religion. His temper was irritable; his disposition unforgiving, or, in his own words, "too keen and revengeful."[4]

Wesley's irritable disposition was a sign to him that something was not right with his situation. The time came when he was called upon to answer some severe charges levied against the Dissenters. In preparation, he examined the indictments with great diligence.

What Wesley discovered during his studies greatly disturbed him. His careful inquiry made him realize that he did not agree with many of the political and religious

---

[4]Kirk, 55.

views held by his friends and colleagues. He began to doubt if he was "in the right."

About this same time, a close friend approached him and "gave him such arguments against that schism with which he was then embarked, as added weight to his reflection when he began to think of leaving it."[5]

This experience lead young Samuel into a time of intense soul-searching. He soon emerged from this period and "renounced the dissenters and attached himself to the Established Church." What Wesley finally concluded was that he was living "in groundless separation from the Established Church."

At the time of his decision, Samuel and Susanna knew each other. He had been a frequent guest in her home and had been a good friend of her father. Because of this, previous biographers have speculated that Samuel influenced Susanna's decision to join the Established Church.

There is little doubt that the two of them discussed the matter together. However, from what is known about Susanna and from what she herself wrote about the religious controversy, it is unlikely that Samuel played a very significant role in her decision.

It is clear from both of their writings that they studied the matter quite diligently on their own. Their letters do not give even a hint of evidence that they influenced each other's decision. We must therefore conclude that their minds were made up primarily on the basis of solid intellectual inquiry.

However, Susanna's letters do confirm that Samuel Wesley played a significant role in rescuing her from the Socinian heresy. Shortly after she made the decision to join the Church of England, Susanna was attracted to Socinianism and led astray. Her faith was shaken and for a time she doubted the truthfulness of the Gospel. Because

---

[5]Kirk, 55–56.

of Samuel, however, her spiritual wanderings were brief.

Samuel was well-versed in the Socinian heresy. During his career at the dissenting academy, he was hired to translate the writings of John Biddle, the father of English Socinianism. When he came to realize the nature of Biddle's beliefs, he refused to finish the job.

Nevertheless, this gave him a good understanding of Socinian beliefs and doctrines. Reflecting on her experience with Socinianism, Susanna was thankful to be "married to a religious orthodox man; by him first drawn off from the Socinian heresy, and afterward confirmed and strengthened by Bishop Bull."

Though no letters confirm it, Samuel and Susanna must have kept in touch during his stay at Oxford. He left for this institution in August 1683, shortly after his life-changing decision to become a member of the Church of England.

Being poor and fatherless, Wesley had to work his way through Oxford by tutoring and writing. Upon graduation in June 1688, he returned to London, was ordained a priest, and was quickly given a curacy that paid him thirty pounds a year.

Just five months after Samuel left Oxford, in November 1688, he and Susanna were married. There is no other explanation for this relatively short courtship except that through the exchange of letters while he was away at Oxford they realized their love for each other.

Perhaps it was the many things that Samuel and Susanna shared in common that attracted them to each other. They both came from strong dissenting family backgrounds. They both made the decision to leave the faith of their youth and to become members of the Church of England. They both had strong, determined personalities.

This is not to say that there were no differences between them. In fact, the extraordinary ways in which they differed has caused some previous biographers to conclude that from the beginning their relationship was buffeted by tension and conflict.

On the one hand, Samuel possessed a hearty sense of humor. He loved to laugh and tell jokes. He was extroverted, witty, and impulsive. His thoughts were often expressed in rhyme and meter. Susanna, on the other hand, was introverted, withdrawn, and spent very little time meditating on humorous things. She was circumspect and methodical in all her ways. Though she was passionate, she kept her emotions in check.

There is little doubt that the similarities and differences between these two personalities caused them to clash. But in the end no one could legitimately question the depth of their love for each other. Biographer Maldwyn Edwards summed up their relationship in this way:

> What happens when the weight moving with irresistible force encounters the immovable obstacle? . . . When the fiery temper of the husband is met by the quiet, unmoving patience and determination of a wife, disagreement amounting at times to a quarrel will certainly result. . . . It is true that Susanna bemoaned on one occasion that Samuel and she rarely agreed on a particular matter, but that was because two more than ordinary people, independent in judgment and of strong convictions, were not willing to disguise their proper views just to flatter the other. Their honesty and integrity, lacking all subtlety, might at times breed dissension, but at least there was no sleep of death; no sacrifice of individuality.[6]

That Samuel greatly loved and respected Susanna is well attested in many of his letters. But his most revealing tribute to her is found in his *Life of Christ*, a work he dedicated to Queen Mary. They had been married only

---

[6]Maldwyn Edwards, *Family Circle* (London: The Epworth Press, 1949), 46.

four years at the time he penned these words:

> The graced my humble roof, and blest my life,
> Blest me by a far greater name than wife;
> Yet still I bore an undisputed sway,
> Nor was't her task, but pleasure, to obey;
> Scarce thought, much less could act, what I denied,
> In our low house there was no room for pride;
> Nor need I e'er direct what still was right,
> She studied my convenience and delight.
> Nor did I for her care ungrateful prove,
> But only used my power to show my love.
> Whate'er she asked I gave, without reproach or
>   grudge,
> For still she reason asked, and I was judge.
> All my commands, requests at her fair hands,
> And her requests to me were all commands.
> To others' thresholds rarely she'd incline.
> Her house her pleasure was, and she was mine;
> Rarely abroad, or never, but with me,
> Or when by pity called, or charity.[7]

For Susanna, the mother of his many children, Samuel had nothing but praise. In a letter to his oldest son, Samuel, while he was a student at Westminster School, the elder Samuel exhorted him to cherish his mother:

September 1706

You know what you owe to one of the best of mothers. Perhaps you may have read of one of the Ptolemies, who chose the name of Philmeter as a more glorious title than if he had assumed that of his predecessor Alexander. And it would be an honest and virtuous ambition in you to attempt to imitate him, for which you have so much reason. Often reflect on the tender and peculiar love which your dear mother has always expressed toward you; the deep affliction of both body and mind

---

[7]Ibid., 48–49.

which she underwent for you, both before and after your birth; the particular care she took of your education when she struggled with so many pains and infirmities; and, above all, the wholesome and sweet motherly advice and counsel which she has often given you to fear God, to take care of your soul as well as of your learning, and to shun all vicious and bad examples. You will, I verily believe, remember that these obligations of gratitude, love, and obedience, and the expressions of them are not confined to your tender years, but must last to the very close of life, and, even after that, render her memory most dear and precious to you.

You will not forget to evidence this by supporting and comforting her in her age, if it please God that she should ever attain to it (though I doubt she will not), and doing nothing which may justly displease or grieve her, or show you unworthy of such a mother. You will endeavor to repay her prayers for you by doubling yours for her; and, above all things, to live such a virtuous and religious life that she may find that her care and love have not been lost upon you, but that we may all meet in heaven.

In short, reverence and love her as much as you will, which I hope will be as much as you can. For though I should be jealous of any other rival in your heart, yet I will not be jealous of her; the more duty you pay her, and the more frequently and kindly you write to her, the more you will please your affectionate father, Samuel Wesley[8]

There came a time when Samuel Wesley was asked by Susanna's brother, Samuel Annesley, to oversee some business transactions for his East India Company. Samuel took on the task but was a miserable failure at it. Annesley, in turn, wrote Samuel a searing letter criticizing his efforts.

---

[8]Ibid., 49–50.

In a beautiful display of love and pride for her husband, Susanna wrote to her brother answering one by one all of his charges against him. She did this by recounting all of Wesley's positive qualities. In this letter, she proved herself to be her husband's greatest, most loving advocate:

January 20, 1722

"Where he lives, I will live, and where he dies, will I die and there will I be buried. God do so unto me and more also if aught but death part him and me."

"My brother-in-law has one invincible obstacle to my business, his distance from London."—Sir, you may please to remember, I put you in mind of this long since.

"Another hindrance, I think he is too zealous for the party he fancies in the right; and has unluckily to do with the opposite faction."—Whether those you employ are factious or not, I'll not determine; but very sure I am, Mr. Wesley is not so; he is zealous in a good cause, as every one ought to be, but the farthest from being a party man of any man in the world.

"Another hindrance is, he knows nothing of these matters."—That is a hindrance indeed, and ought to have been considered on both sides before he entered on your business; for I am verily persuaded that that, and that alone, has been the cause of any mistakes or inadvertency he has been guilty of, and the true reason why God has not blessed him with desired success.

"He trusts in deceitful promises."—But it is a righteous error, and I hope God will forgive us all.

"He wants Mr. Eaton's thrift."—This I can readily believe.

"He is not fit for worldly business."—This I likewise believe, and must own I was mistaken when I did think him fit for it: my own experience has convinced me that he is one of those who, our Savior said, "are not so wise in their generation as the children of the world." And did I not know that the Almighty has His ways, in fixing the bounds of our habitation, which are out of our ken, I should think it awful that a man of his brightness, and rare endowments of learning and useful knowledge, in relation to the church of God, should be confined to an obscure corner of the country, where his talents are buried, and he determined to a way of life for which he is not so well qualified as I could wish. . . .[9]

Susanna eloquently defended her husband's abilities by pointing out that God had ordained him for religion, not for worldly business. Far from being ashamed of her husband's apparent failure, Susanna, throughout her letter, shows her pride in his rare intellectual talents.

These words, which came from Samuel's and Susanna's own pen, reveal their passion for one another (though they had their share of quarrels and disagreements): "The children grew up against the secure unchanging background of their parents' mutual love."[10]

However, there was a time when that love was severely tested. The solid foundation of their relationship was shaken and their marriage was brought to the brink of collapse.

---

[9]Ibid., 51.
[10]Ibid., 52.

4

Tears of Joy and Sorrow

After Samuel had spent only a year at his London curacy, he took a position as chaplain aboard a navy vessel headed for the Irish Sea. The primary reason for this change was financial. The curacy paid him thirty pounds a year, while the chaplain position promised him seventy pounds per annum.

But due to the deplorable conditions on the ship, Samuel did not stay long in that position either. He was "almost starved and poisoned, the captain for a great part of the time keeping no table, nor had we either fish, or butter, or cheese in the ship, and our beef stunk intolerably."[1]

Samuel returned home to London where Susanna was living in a boardinghouse. He had no consistent income but did manage to support them through some literary endeavors. However, with Susanna pregnant with their first child and close to delivery, they decided to move in with her father.

On February 10, 1690, in the home of her girlhood, Susanna gave birth to her first son. They named him Samuel after his father and grandfather. The Wesleys then returned to their boardinghouse in London where

---

[1]*Samuel Wesley's Autobiography*, Ms RAWL. C. 406, Bodleian Library, Oxford University, 3.

Samuel continued to earn a living by writing.

Feeling the financial pinch, Wesley began looking for more work. In June 1690 he was offered the rectorship of St. Leonard's Church, South Ormsby, Lincolnshire. The position promised a steady income of fifty pounds a year. Seeing it as a good opportunity, Samuel immediately took it.

But the move to South Ormsby brought Wesley more financial problems. He spoke of the difficulties he experienced in his autobiography:

> I met with no inconsiderable difficulties in getting there, lying sometimes money-bound here in town, being also indebted for my wife's board and my own. . . . I could not have moved had not my patroness graciously offered to furnish me with what money I wanted on my note to repay it. Accordingly, I had ten pounds when I set out with my family, and ten more when I came to house-keeping.[2]

The South Ormsby rectory was quite primitive and lacking in many worldly comforts. Samuel, using poetic rhyme, described the living conditions in this way:

In a mean cot, composed of reeds and clay,
Wasting in sighs the uncomfortable day:
Near where the inhospitable river mouth roars,
Devouring by degrees the neighboring shores.
Let earth go where it will, I'll not repine,
Nor can unhappy be, while Heaven is mine[3]

Along with his clerical duties, Samuel continued in the ministry of writing. He published two books while at South Ormsby, an essay on all sorts of learning and a discourse concerning the antiquity and authority of Hebrew

---

[2]*Samuel Wesley's Autobiography*, 1.
[3]Kirk, 65.

vowel points. He was also a regular contributor to the *Athenian Gazette*, a biweekly journal published by his brother-in-law, John Dunton.

In 1691 Susanna gave birth to their second child, a daughter, and they named her Susanna. In 1692 she had another daughter whom she named Emilia. Besides the physical strain of constant childbirth, Susanna was also at this time stricken with rheumatism, a painful disease of the joints and muscles.

It was about this time that Susanna realized her first-born son, Samuel, may have a speech problem. He was three and a half years old and had never uttered a word. All hopes of his following in his father's footsteps into ministry were dashed to the ground.

One day, however, Susanna was going through the house looking for young Samuel. When she could not find him anywhere in the house, she went searching through the yard. Though convinced he could not hear, she frantically called out his name. Finally, much to Susanna's surprise and joy, Samuel answered her with clear, intelligible words, "Here I am, Mama." From that time forward, he talked as normally as any other boy his age. Unfortunately, not all of Susanna's trials had such a happy ending.

Her two-year-old daughter, Susanna, had been ill for several months. After the doctors did all they could do for her, little Susanna worsened until finally, in 1694, she died. This was a heart-wrenching experience for Susanna.

Sadly, this was not the only time this mother's eyes would fill with tears over the death of a child. Susanna was to have the unpleasant duty of burying nine of her nineteen children. Most of them died well before the age of maturity.

Late in 1694, Susanna gave birth to twin boys and named them Annesley and Jedediah. But after only one month, these two little ones perished. She had not even recovered from the loss of little Susanna when she had to say good-bye to these sons.

A ray of sunlight came into her life, however, when, in 1695, she gave birth to a healthy baby girl. She named this little one Susanna (Sukey) after her deceased daughter.

In 1696 Susanna welcomed her seventh child, Mary, into the world. She was the last little Wesley to be born in South Ormsby. In 1697 she gave birth to Hetty at Epworth, where Samuel was the newly appointed rector and where he would remain for the rest of his days.

Queen Mary awarded Samuel this position after he dedicated to her his work on the life of Christ. He thought the move to Epworth would improve their situation in at least two ways. First, his salary would increase from fifty pounds a year to 200 per annum.

Secondly, the Epworth rectory was much larger and more suitable for his growing family. But, for both Samuel and Susanna, Epworth turned out to be a place of constant hardship. Mounting debts, dilapidated buildings, and at least one child added to the household per year took a heavy toll on this couple.

It was at this point that the Wesleys went through a crisis that nearly destroyed their marriage. A few years after he took over the Epworth parish, Samuel became deeply distraught over his financial situation.

Realizing his need for help, he wrote the following letter to Dr. Sharpe, Archbishop of York:

December 28, 1700

I must own that I am ashamed . . . to confess that I am three hundred pounds in debt, when I have a living of which I have made two hundred pounds per annum, though I could hardly let it now for eight score.

I doubt not one reason of my being sunk so far is my

not understanding worldly affairs, and my aversion to law. . . .

It will be no great wonder that when I had but fifty pounds per annum for six or seven years together, and nothing to begin the world with, one child at least per annum, and my wife sick for half that time, that I should run one hundred and fifty pounds in debt. . . .

When I had the rectory at Epworth given me, my Lord of Sarum was so generous as to pass his word to his banker for one hundred pounds, which I borrowed of him. It cost me very little less than fifty pounds of this in my journey to London, and getting into my living . . . and with the other fifty pounds I stopped the mouths of my most importunate creditors.

When I removed to Epworth I was forced to take up fifty pounds more, for setting up a farm . . . and buying some part of what was necessary toward furnishing my house, which was larger, as well as my family. . . .

The next year my barn fell, which cost me forty pounds in rebuilding . . . and having an aged mother who would have gone to prison if I had not assisted her, she cost me upwards of forty pounds, which obliged me to take up another fifty pounds. I have had three more children since I came here three years ago and another one on the way, and my wife incapable of any business in my family, as she has been for almost a quarter of a year; yet we have but one maidservant, to reduce all possible expenses. . . .

Fifty pounds of interest and principal I have paid my Lord of Sarum's banker. All which together keeps me needy, especially since interest money begins to pinch me. . . . Humbly asking pardon for this tedious trouble,

I am your grace's most obliged and
humble servant, Samuel Wesley[4]

The archbishop responded to Samuel's urgent plea for

[4]Arnold Dallimore, *Susanna Wesley: The Mother of John & Charles Wesley* (Grand Rapids: Baker Book House, 1993), 44–45.

help by giving him 185 pounds. Wesley was undoubtedly thankful for Dr. Sharpe's generosity. At the same time, however, he must have felt a tinge of humiliation for having to appeal to a superior for financial aid.

In 1701 Susanna gave birth to a second set of twins, a boy and a girl. These precious babies must have died shortly after birth because they were never named. Sometime in 1702, she had another baby girl and named her Anne.

Meanwhile, Samuel became increasingly distressed over his financial situation and the growing pressures at home. One night, during the evening prayers, he noticed that Susanna did not say "Amen" to his prayers for King William. This so incensed Samuel that he vowed never to sleep with her again. He eventually mounted his horse and left her.

Samuel used this "prayer" incident as justification for leaving his wife in such perilous times. However, considering their dire circumstances, the more likely reason why he left had to do with his desire to escape the many pressures and responsibilities that were placed on him at home.

Susanna's refusal to acknowledge his prayer merely gave Samuel the way out he was looking for. The fact of the matter is that this was certainly not the first time she refused to say "Amen" to such a prayer. It was simply the occasion Wesley chose to do something about it.

It is important to understand that Susanna did not act this way merely to spite her husband. Her actions sprang from her well-thought-out convictions. The reason Susanna refused to acknowledge Samuel's prayer for King William was because she did not believe he had the right to the throne.

In 1688 England had gone through a revolution in which King James II of England was exiled and his daughter Mary was made queen. Her husband, William, was then brought over from Holland and declared king.

Because William was not a true Englishman, a great number of English people, including Susanna, refused to recognize him as their king. Those who held this position were known as "nonjurors."

The king held jurisdiction over the clergy and was the one who appointed them to church positions. Thus, besides his desire to escape from the ever-increasing pressures at home, Samuel saw Susanna's refusal to acknowledge King William as a threat to his advancement in the church.

Samuel thought his leaving Susanna would assure the king, if he ever heard of Susanna's conduct, that he did not approve of his wife's beliefs.

Some previous biographers have doubted the validity of this entire incident. However, there is compelling evidence to support it. First, though he was not born yet, John Wesley mentions the event in some of his writings.[5]

Secondly, in 1953, some letters written by Susanna in 1702 surfaced.[6] In them, she not only confirms that this incident took place but she also reveals the emotional turmoil she experienced during this trying time.

In the following letter addressed to Lady Yarborough, a fellow nonjuror, Susanna described her desperate situation and asked for her guidance.

To the Lady Yarborough
Saturday night, March 7, 1702
Madam,

I am definitely obliged to you for your charming civility to a person so utterly unworthy of your favors, but oh, madam! I must tell your ladyship that you have somewhat mistaken my case. You advise me to continue with my husband, and God knows how gladly I would do

---

[5]Ibid., 47.
[6]Ibid., 47–54.

it, but there, there is my supreme affliction, he will not live with me. 'Tis but a little while since he one evening observed in our family prayers that I did not say Amen to his prayer for KW [King William] as I usually do to all others; upon which he retired to his study, and calling me to him asked the reason of my not saying Amen to the prayer. I was a little surprised at the question and don't know well what I answered, but too well I remember what followed: he immediately kneeled down and imprecated the divine vengeance upon himself and all his posterity if ever he touched me more or came into a bed with me before I had begged God's pardon and his for not saying Amen to the prayer for the king.

This, madam, is my unhappy case. I've unsuccessfully represented to him the unlawfulness and unreasonableness of his oath; that the man in that case has no more power over his own body than the woman over hers; that since I'm willing to let him quietly enjoy his opinions, he ought not to deprive me of my little liberty of conscience. But he has opened his mouth to the Lord and what help? ... I have no resentment against my master, so far from it that the very next day I went with him to the Communion, though he that night forsook my bed, to which he has been a stranger ever since.

I'm almost ashamed to own what extreme disturbance this accident has given me, yet I value not the world. I value neither reputation, friends, or anything in comparison of the single satisfaction of preserving a conscience void of offense toward God and man; and how I can do that if I mock Almighty God for what I think is no sin, is past my discerning. But I am inexpressibly miserable, for I can see no possibility of reconciling these differences, though I would submit to anything or do anything in the world to oblige him to live in the house with me.

I appeal to your ladyship if my circumstances are not strangely unhappy. I don't think there's any precedent for such a case in the whole world; and may I not say as the prophet, I am the person that has seen affliction. I'm almost afraid I've already complied with him too far, but most humbly beg your ladyship's direction.[7]

Lady Yarborough shared Susanna's plight with a friend who quickly agreed that her position was correct. On 5 April 1702, Wesley left for London. He was apparently going there to explain the entire situation to the Archbishop of York and Bishop of Lincoln.

Susanna then headed for the home of Lady Yarborough. While she was there she wrote a letter to another leading nonjuror, Bishop Hickes. She told him about her circumstances and asked for his direction.

She also informed him that her husband was "referring the whole matter to the Archbishop of York and Bishop Lincoln, and says if I will not be persuaded by them, he will do anything rather than live with a person that is the declared enemy of his country."

Bishop Hickes was filled with much compassion and pity for Susanna. He wrote her that he was "persuaded if it were represented to the two persons to whom you say Mr. Wesley will refer it, that they would pity you and blame his conduct, and tell him that his oath lays no obligation upon him, but that of repentance for its rashness and iniquity of it."[8]

Susanna received Bishop Hickes' letter of encouragement just when she was at her lowest point. On July 31, 1702, she wrote him the following letter:

Bishop Hickes,
. . . My master was then at London and had given me time to consider what to do, whether I would submit to his judgment and implicitly obey him in matters of conscience. I foresaw a great many evils would inevitably

[7]Ibid., 48–49.
[8]Ibid., 50.

befall me if I refused to satisfy his desires, and had scarcely enough courage to support me when your letter came, which was the noblest cordial and gave me the greatest satisfaction in my whole life.

When he returned he absolutely refused a reference. . . . He stayed two days and then left me early one morning with a resolution never to see me more. But the infinite Power that disposes and overrules the minds of men as he pleases . . . so ordered it that in his way he met a clergyman to whom he communicated his intentions, and the reason that induced him to leave his family: he extremely pitied him and condemned me, but, however, he encouraged him to return home.

But as often happens . . . his long absence occasioned abundance of trouble to himself and his family . . . as strange a complication of misfortunes as perhaps ever happened to any persons in the world. . . .

Before I've finished my letter I'm alarmed by a new misfortune: my house is caught on fire by one of my servants, I think not carelessly but by so odd an accident as I may say of it, as the magicians said of Moses' fourth miracle, this is the finger of God. Two thirds are burnt, and most of our goods are utterly spoiled. May heaven avert all evil from my children and grant that the heavy curse my master has wished upon himself and family may terminate in this life. I most earnestly beg your prayers, that God at last have mercy upon us, at least that he would spare the innocent children, however he is pleased to deal with the unhappy parents.

I am, sir,

Your most obliged humble servant,

S. Wesley[9]

When the fire that Susanna referred to in her letter broke out, Samuel was on his way to London. When he was informed that it was his house on fire, he got on a

---

[9]Ibid., 52–53.

horse and returned home. The reality that he nearly lost his entire family must have brought Samuel to his senses.

He stayed there at Epworth, repaired the house, and resumed his clerical duties. Susanna never did change her mind about the king. But apparently that did not matter.

From what is known about the Wesleys' relationship from this point forward, it is clear that they put this entire incident behind them. They forgave each other and wholeheartedly renewed their love for each other.

Apart from this incident, "we do not know of any quarrel which threatened the very security of the family."[10] Their marriage withstood this fiery trial and, in the long run, it made them stronger to face the many hardships which were still to come.

In 1703 their renewed commitment produced one of their most famous sons, John Wesley. This precious little boy was the focus of one of the Wesleys' most severe trials. Young John almost perished in the famous blaze of 1709, which destroyed all of the Wesleys' possessions.

Needless to say, this fire had a profound effect on Susanna. Not only did she lose all her material goods but she nearly had to watch her little son be swallowed up in the flames.

In the following letter written to a clergyman, Susanna chronicled the events that took place that cold February night.

Epworth, August 24, 1709
On Wednesday night, February 9, between the hours of eleven and twelve, some sparks fell from the roof of our house, upon one of the children's (Hetty's) feet. She immediately ran to our chamber, and called us. Mr. Wesley, hearing a cry of fire in the street, started up, (as I

---

[10]Edwards, 48.

was very ill, he lay in a separate room from me) and, opening his door found the fire was in his own house. He immediately came to my room, and bid me and my two eldest daughters rise quickly and shift for ourselves. Then he ran and burst open the nursery door, and called to the maid to bring out the children. The two little ones lay in the bed with her; the three others in another bed. She snatched up the youngest, and bid the rest follow; which the three elder did. When we were got into the hall, and were surrounded with flames, Mr. Wesley found he had left the keys of the doors above the stairs. He ran up, and recovered them, a minute before the staircase took fire. When we opened the street door, the strong northeast wind drove the flames in with such violence, that none could stand against them. But some of our children got out through the windows, the rest through a little door in the garden. I was not in a condition to climb up to the windows; (she was 8–9 months pregnant) neither could I get to the garden door. I endeavored three times to force my passage through the street door, but was often beat back by the fury of the flames. In this distress, I besought our blessed Savior for help, and then waded through the fire, naked as I was, which did me no further harm than a little scorching of my hands and face.

When Mr. Wesley had seen the other children safe, he heard the child (John) in the nursery cry. He attempted to go up the stairs, but they were all on fire and would not bear his weight. Finding it impossible to give any help, he kneeled down in the hall, and recommended the soul of the child to God.[11]

Young John Wesley was finally saved through the quick-thinking efforts of a neighbor. John stood near a window and the man set him on his shoulders and carried him to safety. Had it not been for this man's heroic ef-

[11]Donald L. Kline, *Susanna Wesley: God's Catalyst for Revival* (Lima: The C.S.S. Publishing Co., 1980), 4–5.

forts, the name Wesley would not be as well known as it is today.

This event brought Susanna many tears of joy and sorrow. Words could not express the joy she felt as she held her son safely in her arms, freshly plucked from the blaze.

But sorrow upon sorrow weighed heavily upon her when she realized that everything she owned was gone, including her books, her writings, her teaching manuals, and her treasured family papers.

However, through all these trials, Susanna never uttered a bitter word toward God. In a letter written to John several years later, she said, "It is certainly true that I have had large experience of what the world calls adverse fortune. . . .

"Yet I dare not presume, nor do I despair, but rather leave it to our almighty Savior to do with me both in life and death just what He pleases, for I have no choice."[12]

Susanna Wesley had learned to trust God in all situations. Still, she had to wonder what caused this blaze. This one was not like the fire of 1702, which occurred in the middle of summer during the dry season.

This fire happened in the dead of winter and in the middle of the night. The oven flames, which were the usual cause of house fires, had been extinguished for hours. Everyone in the house, including the servants, were sound asleep.

But the most peculiar thing about this fire was that it did not start in any of the lower rooms. The initial sparks came from the roof. These circumstances taken together must have caused Susanna to suspect that this devastating fire was anything but an accident.

---

[12]Ibid., 33–34.

5

The Tale of Old Jeffery

The sound of rushing winds. Strange knockings in rhythmic patterns of three. A man crying out in agony as if he was in the throes of death. The sound of footsteps moving rapidly up and down the staircase. Obnoxious noises underneath the beds and in empty rooms.

"Gobblings like a turkey. . . . Casements clattered. Warming pans and every vessel of brass and iron rang out a discord of strange sounds. Latches moved up and down with uncommon swiftness. Without the touch of human hand, doors flew open, banged, and violently pushed against those who sought to pass from one room to another."[1]

It all started one December night in 1715. The Wesley home had become inundated with strange noises. At first it was only the servants and the children who experienced these peculiar happenings.

One of the new servants claimed she heard in the middle of the night a man crying out in horrible pain. Then Sukey and Anne claimed they heard strange knockings in patterns of three. Emilia said she heard the sound of breaking glass in the kitchen. But when she went to

---

[1]Kirk, 97.

investigate, there was nothing broken.

A male servant swore he heard the sound of someone going up and down the stairs dragging his nightgown and gobbling like a turkey. This series of strange events was only the beginning of the terrifying things that took place in the Wesley home.

"The house shook from top to bottom. The sleeping children began to moan and sweat. The wind rose, whistled, and howled in dismal cadences."[2] Besides all of this, there were some frightening visible manifestations.

The same male servant who heard the turkey gobble also thought he saw "something like a small rabbit coming out of the copper hole. . . . It turned round five times very swiftly."[3] He tried to catch the animal, but it vanished before his eyes.

Up to this point, neither Samuel nor Susanna had heard or seen anything. Then one night Emilia brought Susanna into her room where she heard noises coming from underneath the bed. Susanna also saw something like a badger without a head run across the room and disappear.

Belief in ghosts was quite prevalent among the people of England in that day. Susanna was convinced that an obnoxious ghost had taken up residence in their home and was frolicking in their midst. There was also a strong belief that ghosts foretold the death of the one in the household who could not hear it.

Fearing for her husband's life, Susanna informed Samuel of these events. She also shared with him her belief that the house was haunted. Wesley, however, did not agree with her interpretation.

He reportedly said, "Sukey, I am ashamed of you. These boys and girls frighten one another; but you are a

---

[2]Kirk, 98.
[3]Kirk, 99.

woman of sense and should know better. Let me hear of it no more."[4] Susanna was unquestionably upset by her husband's unbelieving attitude and rude comments.

However, Wesley's disposition quickly changed when the very next night he was awakened by the sound of nine loud knocks. Susanna was relieved that he had finally experienced the strange phenomenon and that he was determined to do something about it.

On one occasion, the freakish noises interrupted the night with an unspeakable vengeance. The disturbance became so loud that both Samuel and Susanna found it impossible to sleep. The two of them arose and went from room to room, searching for what was causing the noises. But they saw nothing, and the strange sounds always seemed to be coming from the room they had just left.

Samuel soon became as frequently disturbed by these occurrences as the rest of his family. One night he became so annoyed that he cried out, "Thou deaf and dumb spirit, why dost thou frighten children that cannot answer thee? Come to me in my study that am a man!"[5]

The spirit quickly obliged Wesley by responding with the same peculiar knock he himself used when he wanted to let Susanna know it was him at the outside gate. From this time forward, the rector was constantly harassed in his study.

On one occasion, Wesley began to fear for his son Samuel, who was in London. He became convinced that the spirit was foretelling his death. So he called out, "If thou art the spirit of my son Samuel, I pray thee knock three knocks and no more."[6] But the spirit never replied.

These peculiar visitations went on in the Wesley home for a little over two months. This was enough time for the younger children to cease being frightened by

[4]Kirk, 100.
[5]Dallimore, 82.
[6]Dallimore, 83.

them and to start joking about them. They named the
spirit "Old Jeffery," after the former rector of Epworth.

"When the gentle tappings at the bed's head began,
they would say, 'Old Jeffery is coming; it is time to go to
sleep!' When the noises were heard in the daytime, little
Kezzy chased the sounds from room to room, desiring no
better amusement than to hear the mysterious answers
to the stamp of her own foot."[7]

Because the tale of Old Jeffery is so well documented
by nearly all the Wesley family members, no previous biographer has seriously doubted the validity of the incident. There is, however, a considerable controversy over
the exact cause of the strange events.

Because belief in superstitions and ghosts were so
prevalent in that day, many previous biographers were
not willing to give much credence to the Wesleys' explanations of supernatural origins.

According to Dallimore, these writers explained "Old
Jeffery" as a product of natural means:

> Coleridge discovers in the Wesley family "an angry
> and damnatory predetermination" to believe in the
> ghost. . . . Dr. Salmon accuses Hetty Wesley of playing
> tricks on her family and producing all the noises. . . .
> Priestly offers the theory of imposture by servants and
> neighbors; Isaac Taylor resolves "Old Jeffery" into a
> monkey-like "performing droll" of a spirit. Mr. Wesley
> had preached for several Sundays against the "cunning
> men" of the neighborhood whom the ignorant peasants
> used to consult as wizards; and Andrew Lang thinks the
> performances of "Old Jeffery" were the revenge taken by
> these "cunning men."[8]

Despite the rationality of these explanations, there is
no good reason for dismissing the Wesley family's claims

---

[7]Kirk, 101.
[8]Dallimore, 86.

of the supernatural origin of Old Jeffery.

The personal testimony of Emilia Wesley alone, who was a skeptic herself, is enough to give credence to their beliefs.

> I am so far from being superstitious, that I was too much inclined to infidelity; so that I heartily rejoice at having such an opportunity of convincing myself, past doubt or scruple, of the existence of some beings besides those we see. A whole month was sufficient to convince anybody of the reality of the thing (Old Jeffery), and to try all ways of discovering any trick, had it been possible for any such to have been used.[9]

It is clear, therefore, that the antics of Old Jeffery cannot be blamed on belligerent neighbors or cunning men. There is, however, an event that took place at the Wesley home that can easily be traced back to these men: the fire of 1709.

Far from being an accident, there is ample evidence to support the idea that the fire of 1709, which destroyed all of the Wesleys' earthly possessions, was deliberately ignited by wicked men and ungrateful neighbors.

In order to understand what would lead these men to commit such an evil crime, we must go back to the general election of 1705. As we have seen in previous chapters, the Church of England was intimately involved with the government and deeply concerned about political issues.

The cry had gone out from the press that the Established Church was in grave danger. Rumor had it that it was going to be given over into the hands of the Dissenters. Many High Church clergymen moved into action by sounding the alarm from their pulpits and exhorting their parishioners to fight for the Church.

---

[9]Kirk, 108.

Those who were seeking political offices took advantage of the upheaval. Sir John Thorold and "Champion" Dymoke sought reelection to Parliament, while Colonels Whichcott and Bertie were seeking to take their seats.

Because of their numerous freehold voters, the Isle of Axholme, where Epworth was located, was extremely important to political candidates. According to Kirk, those candidates who won over the men of Isle would win the election.[10]

Being the rector of Epworth and the leading religious authority on the Isle of Axholme, Samuel Wesley was heavily courted by both Thorold and Dymoke and by Whichcott and Bertie. The former were open supporters of the Royalty and the Church of England.

The latter claimed to be aligned with the Established Church but were more quiet about their allegiance. Wesley promised Thorold that he would not vote against him. But he adamantly refused to support Dymoke.

However, because he and Whichcott had developed a good relationship, Wesley promised him his "vote and interest." Once he made known his political allegiance, Wesley took a short trip to London. When he returned a few weeks later, he did not find things as they were.

Whichcott and Bertie had turned against the Church and had sided with the Dissenters. Wesley then withdrew his support for Whichcott and quickly voted for Thorold. This so infuriated the men of the Isle, who supported Whichcott, that violent protests broke out at the Epworth rectory.

Samuel wrote the following letter to Archbishop Sharpe describing the terrible trials that had come upon him and his family as a result of his decision:

---

[10]Kirk, 88.

Epworth, June 7, 1705

I went to Lincoln on Tuesday night, May 29, and the election began on Wednesday, 30. A great part of the night our Isle people kept drumming, shouting and firing pistols and guns under the window where my wife lay, who had been brought to bed not three weeks. I had put the child with his nurse across from our house; the noise kept his nurse awake till one or two in the morning. Then they left off and his nurse, being heavy with sleep, overlaid the child. She waked, and finding it dead, ran over to my house almost distracted, and calling my servants, threw it into their arms. They, as wise as she, ran with it to my wife, and before she was well awake, threw it cold and dead into her arms. She composed herself as well as she could, and that day got it buried.

A clergyman met me in the castle yard, and told me to withdraw, for the Isle men intended to hurt me. Another told me he had heard near twenty of them say, "If they got me in the castle yard they would squeeze me guts out". . . . I went home by Gainsbro' and God preserved me.

When they knew I was home, they sent the drum and mob, with guns, etc., to disturb me till after midnight. One of them, passing by on Friday evening and seeing my children in the yard cried out, "O ye devils! We will come and turn ye all out of doors a-begging shortly." God convert them and forgive them!

All this, thank God, does not in the least sink my wife's spirits. For my own, I feel them disturbed and disordered. . . .

S. Wesley

By this time, Susanna had already buried several of her children, whose lives were cut short due to either illness or premature birth. But because of the bizarre circumstances surrounding the death of this child, this loss must have been especially difficult for her.

Susanna Wesley and her children had to endure many

more acts of cruelty from the townspeople. Their fields were set on fire, their cattle were stabbed and nearly bled to death, and their dog's leg was brutally cut.

The angry men of the Isle continued to make life miserable for the Wesleys. They shouted out obscenities to them and fired their guns in front of their home during all hours of the night. The children rarely ventured out of the house for fear they might be shot.

To add to all of this, a creditor by the name of Pinder, a supporter of Colonel Whichcott, had Wesley arrested because he owed him thirty pounds. Wesley wrote another letter to Dr. Sharpe from his prison cell in Lincoln castle. In it he explained the awful plight of his wife and children.

> I thank God my wife was pretty well recovered, and churched some days before I was taken from her. . . . One of my biggest concerns was my being forced to leave my poor lambs in the midst of so many wolves. But the Great Shepherd is able to provide for them, and to preserve them. My wife bears it with that courage which becomes her, and which I expected from her. . . .[11]

Susanna found her strength in God and rose to the challenge of being a single mother for a time. She had very little money to live on and was completely dependent upon the produce of the dairy to feed herself and her children.

Still, she was concerned about her husband in prison and feared that he may be worse off than herself. So she sent him her wedding rings in hope that he could sell them, pay off his debt, and be released from prison.

Samuel was deeply moved by his wife's sacrifice but immediately returned the rings to her with the assurance that God would provide for him. Wesley was jailed

---

[11]Dallimore, 68.

in June 1705 and was released sometime before the end of that year.

The rector returned to Epworth to find that many of his parishioners still resented him for his change in political views. His friends urged him to leave Epworth before something terrible happened. But he refused to leave. He gave the following reasons in a letter to Archbishop York:

> I confess that I am not of that mind [to leave], because I may yet do some good there; and 'tis like a coward to desert my post because the enemy fire is thick upon me. They have only wounded me yet, and, I believe, can't kill me.[12]

God honored Samuel Wesley's courage by protecting him from one of his worst enemies, Robert Darwin. In a letter to her son Samuel, Susanna described what happened to this vicious man.

> He was one of the most implacable enemies your father had among his parishioners: one that insulted him most basely in his troubles: one that was ready to do him all the mischief he could, not to mention his affronts to me and the children, and how heartily he wished to see our ruin, which God permitted him not to see. . . . [He fell from his horse and broke his neck] His face was torn to pieces; one of his eyes beat out; his under lip cut off; his nose broken down; and, in short, he was one of the most dreadful examples of the severe justice of God that I have known. . . . This man and one more have been now cut off in the midst of their sins since your father's confinement.[13]

But even after this incident, the parishioners contin-

---

[12]Kirk, 94.
[13]Kirk, 94–95.

ued to attack the Wesley family. The neighboring peoples were intent on destroying them, which is what they very nearly did in the fire of 1709. Their goal was to watch the family perish in their parish.

But God foiled the plan of their enemies and allowed the Wesleys to escape the fire with their lives. Now came the task of finding some place for the huge family to live. One of their few friendly neighbors invited Samuel, Susanna, and two-year-old Charles to live with them.

While they were there, the Wesleys welcomed their nineteenth and final child into the world. It was a girl and they named her Kezzy. Hetty and Sukey went to live with their Uncle Matthew in London. The rest of the children were scattered into various homes.

Meanwhile, the hostile people of Epworth rejoiced at the thought of the Wesleys being gone. But much to their chagrin, Samuel returned to the scene of the crime and began construction on a new rectory. He made it larger and more sturdy than the previous rectory and built it with fire-resistant bricks.

Early in 1711, the new rectory at Epworth was finished, and the Wesley family returned home. Samuel and Susanna then set about their business and tried to resume a normal life. Wesley went back to his clerical duties while Susanna watched over the household and the children.

Unfortunately, the tension between the Wesleys and the neighboring peoples also resumed and continued to grow. That is, until 1712, when Susanna shook the gates of hell, and the attitude of the people began to change.

6

The Quickening

Early in 1712, Samuel Wesley left for London to attend a convocation. This gathering of church leaders took place at least twice a year and, although he was not required to attend, Wesley made an effort to be at every meeting. This put a considerable amount of financial stress on the entire family.

First, the cost for Samuel to travel to London was no less than fifty pounds. In addition to this, he had to pay a curate to watch over the parish while he was gone. The convocation of 1712 kept Samuel busy in London for several months.

He entrusted the Epworth parish to Inman, a curate who quickly proved to be unqualified for the task. Not only did he fail to expound from the pulpit the great truths of the Christian faith, but he also obsessively preached on one ethical theme: the pitfalls of being in debt.

He did this because he knew of Samuel's financial problems and sought to blacken his name. The motives behind his actions are not exactly known, but he probably did it to make himself look better in the eyes of the people of Epworth.

Needless to say, Susanna was quite agitated by Inman's unproductive sermons and his lack of respect for her husband. But, besides his inadequacies at the pulpit, Susanna was also upset by Inman's practice of only one church service on Sunday.

With the church service over early on Sunday morning, Susanna feared that her children would have too much idle time on their hands. She was concerned that they would desecrate the Lord's sacred day by giving themselves over to frivolous behavior.

So, in order to make sure that the Sabbaths (Sundays) were upheld in holy behavior, Susanna began holding religious meetings on Sunday evenings. She would gather the children and the servants together in the kitchen and would sing psalms, read prayers, and deliver a sermon taken from Samuel's library.

Before long, some of the people in the community heard about what Susanna was doing and began to attend her meetings. Within a few months, the attendance grew to about thirty or forty people. Soon after this, an extraordinary event took place in Susanna's life, which sparked an incredible religious revival.

Coming across a stirring account of two Danish missionaries and their missionary endeavors in a foreign land, Susanna was so "quickened" by their story that she determined to do something similar for the glory of God. She began by meeting with each of her children on an individual basis. She would talk with each of them about the condition of their soul and about their commitment to God. If her children had any questions about their faith, Susanna would answer them to the best of her ability.

As well, she began to spend more individual time with the neighbors who attended her meetings. She would read to them "the best and most awakening sermons" she could find and then make herself available to answer their questions.

Shortly thereafter, Susanna's Sunday evening meetings had blossomed to a standing-room-only crowd of two hundred people. At this point, she wrote a letter to her husband in London to inform him of her activities. Wesley wrote back to Susanna and expressed many concerns about the meetings and questioned whether they should continue.

In the following eloquent and forthcoming letter, Susanna openly dealt with her husband's concerns. Without showing any disrespect for Samuel's authority, she justified herself and the continuance of the meetings.

Epworth, February 6, 1712

I heartily thank you for dealing so plainly and faithfully with me in a matter of no common concern. The main of your objections against our Sunday evening meetings are, first, that it will look unusual; secondly, my sex; and lastly, our meeting will appear worldly. To all which I shall answer briefly.

As to its looking unusual, I grant it does; and so does almost everything that is serious, or that may in any way advance the glory of God or the salvation of souls, if it be performed out of a pulpit, or in the way of common conversation; because in our corrupt age the utmost care and diligence have been used to banish all discourse of God or spiritual concerns out of society, as if religion were never to appear out of the closet, and we were to be ashamed of nothing so much as of professing ourselves to be Christians.

To your second, I reply, that as I am a woman, so I am also mistress of a large family. And though the superior charge of the souls contained in it lies upon you, as head of the family, and as their minister; yet in your absence I cannot but look upon every soul you leave under my care as a talent committed to me, under a trust, by the great Lord of all the families of heaven and earth. And if I am unfaithful to him, or to you, in neglecting to improve these talents, how shall I answer unto him when he shall command me to render an account of my stewardship?

As these and other such like thoughts made me at first take a more than ordinary care of the souls of my children and servants; so, knowing that our most holy religion requires a strict observation of the Lord's day, and not thinking that we fully answered the end of the institution by only going to church, but that likewise we are obliged to fill up the intermediate spaces of that sacred time by other acts of piety and devotion; I thought it my duty to spend some part of the day in reading to and instructing my family, especially in your absence, when, having no afternoon's service, we have so much leisure for such exercises; and such time I esteemed spent in a way more acceptable to God than if I had retired to my own private devotions.

This was the beginning of my present practice: other people coming in and joining with us was purely accidental. Our servant told his parents—they first desired to be admitted; then others who heard of it begged leave also; so our company increased to about thirty, and seldom exceeded forty last winter; and why it increased since, I leave you to judge after you have read what follows.

Soon after you went to London, Emily found in your study the account of the Danish missionaries, which having never seen, I ordered her to read it to me. I was never, I think, more affected with anything than with the relation of their travels; and was exceeding pleased with the noble design they were engaged in. Their labors refreshed my soul beyond measure; and I could not forbear spending a good part of that evening in praising and adoring the divine goodness for inspiring those good men with such an ardent zeal for his glory, that they were willing to hazard their lives, and all that is esteemed dear to men in this world, to advance the honor of their Master, Jesus. For several days I could think of speaking of little else. At last it came into my mind, though I am not a man nor a minister of the gospel, and so cannot be employed in such a worthy employment as they were; yet, if my heart were sincerely devoted to God, and if I were inspired with a true zeal for his glory, and did really desire the salvation of souls, I might do somewhat more than I do. I thought I might live in a more exemplary manner in some things; I might pray more for the people, and speak with more warmth to those with whom I have an opportunity of conversing. However, I resolved to begin with my own children; and, accordingly, I proposed and observed the following method. I take such a proportion of time as I can best spare every night to discourse with each child by itself, on something that relates to its principal concerns. On Monday I talk with Molly; on Tuesday with Hetty; Wednesday with Nancy; Thursday with Jacky; Friday with Patty; Saturday with Charles; and with Emily and Sukey together, on Sunday.

With those neighbors who then came to me I discoursed more freely and affectionately than before. I chose the best and most awakening sermons we had, and I spent more time with them in such exercises. Since this our company has increased every night, for I dare deny none that ask admittance. Last Sunday, I believe we had above two hundred, and yet many went away for want of room.

But I never dare positively presume to hope that God would make use of me as an instrument in doing good; the furthest I dare go was, it may be: who can tell? With God all things are possible. I will resign myself to him: or, as Herbert better expresses it,

Only since God does often make
Of lowly matter for high uses meet,
I throw me at his feet;
There will I lie until my Maker seek
For some mean stuff, whereon to show his skill;
Then is my time.

And thus I rested, without passing any reflection on

myself, or forming any judgment about the success or event of this undertaking.

Your third objection I leave to be answered by your own judgment. We meet not on any worldly design. We banish all temporal concerns from our society: none is suffered to mingle any discourse about them with our reading or singing: we keep close to the business of the day; and as soon as it is over, they all go home. And where is the harm of this? If I and my children went a visiting on Sunday nights, or if we admitted of impertinent visits, as too many do who think themselves good Christians, perhaps it would be thought no scandalous practice, though in truth it would be so. Therefore, why any should reflect upon you, let your station be what it will, because your wife endeavors to draw people to the church, and to restrain them, by reading and other persuasions, from their profanation of God's most holy day, I cannot conceive. But if any should be so mad as to do it, I wish you would not regard it. For my part, I value no censure on this account. I have long since shook hands with the world, and I heartily wish I had never given them more reason to speak against me.

As for your proposal of letting some other person read. Alas! you do not consider what a people there are. I do not think one man among them could read a sermon, without spelling a good part of it; and how would that edify the rest? Nor has any of our family a voice strong enough to be heard by such a number of people.

But there is one thing about which I am much dissatisfied; that is, their being present at family prayers. I do not speak of any concern I am under, barely because so many are present; for those who have the honor of speaking to the great and holy God need not be ashamed to speak before the whole world; but because of my sex. I doubt if it be proper for me to present the prayer of the people to God.

Last Sunday I would have dismissed them before

prayers; but they begged so earnestly to stay, that I dare
not deny them.[1]

After reading this candid letter, Samuel wrote to Susanna and gave her his approval. She continued the
meetings, and much good was accomplished in the community. The grace of God was evident in the children's
behavior and in the people's speech and conduct.

The curate, Mr. Inman, and a few other men were fu-
rious at Susanna's success. Inman wrote a letter to Samuel accusing Susanna of holding a conventicle, an illegal
religious meeting. Samuel, recalling the days of his Dissenting meetings, once again became alarmed by Susanna's meetings and their implications.

Wesley feared that some of the High Church clergymen in the area would find out about these meetings at
his home and accuse him of defecting to the Dissenters.
A scandal like this would certainly ruin his career. So, he
immediately wrote to Susanna and asked her to stop the
meetings.

Susanna wrote the following reply to her husband.

Epworth, February 25, 1712
    Some days since I received a letter from you I sup-
pose dated the 16th instant, which I made no great haste
to answer, because I judged it necessary for both of us to
take some time to consider before you determine in a
matter of such great importance.

    I shall not inquire how it was possible that you
should be prevailed on by the senseless clamors of two
or three of the worst of your parish, to condemn what you
so lately approved. But I shall tell you my thoughts in
as few words as possible. I do not hear of more than three
or four persons who are against our meeting, of whom
Inman is the chief. He and Whitely, I believe, may call

[1]Adam Clarke, *Memoirs of the Wesley Family* (New York: Lane and
Tippett, 1848), 387–390.

it a conventicle; but we hear no outcry here, nor has any one said a word against it to me. And what does their calling it a conventicle signify? Does it alter the nature of the thing? Or do you think that what they say is a sufficient reason to forbear a thing that has already done much good, and by the blessing of God may do much more? If its being called a conventicle, by those who know in their conscience they misrepresent it, did really make it one, what you say would be somewhat to the purpose; but it is plain in fact that this one thing has brought more people to church than ever anything did in so short a time. We used not to have above twenty to twenty-five at evening service, whereas we have now between two and three hundred; which are more than ever came before to hear Inman in the morning.

Besides the constant attendance on the public worship of God, our meeting has wonderfully conciliated the minds of this people toward us, so that we now live in the greatest amity imaginable; and what is still better, they are very much reformed in their behavior on the Lord's day; and those who used to be playing in the streets now come to hear a good sermon read, which is surely more acceptable to almighty God.

Another reason for what I do is that I have no other way of conversing with this people, and therefore have no other way of doing them good: but by this I have an opportunity of exercising the greatest and noblest charity, that is, charity of their souls.

Some families who seldom went to church, now go constantly; and one person, who had not been there for seven years, is now prevailed upon to go with rest.

There are many other good consequences of this meeting which I have not time to mention. Now, I beseech you, weigh all these things in an impartial balance: on the one side, the honor of almighty God, the doing much good to many souls, and the friendship of the best among whom we live; on the other, (if folly, impiety, and vanity may abide in the scale against so ponderous a weight), the senseless objections of a few scandalous persons, laughing at us, and censuring us as precise and hypocritical; and when you have duly considered all things, let me have your positive determination.

I need not tell you the consequences, if you determine to put an end to our meeting. You may easily perceive what prejudice it may raise in the minds of these people against Inman, especially, who has had so little wit as to speak publicly against it. I can now keep them to the church; but if it be laid aside, I doubt they will ever go to hear him more, at least those who come from the lower end of the town. But if this be continued till you return, which now will not be long, it may please God that their hearts may be so changed by that time, that they may love and delight in his public worship, so as never to neglect it more.

If you do, after all, think fit to dissolve this assembly, do not tell me that you desire me to do it, for that will not satisfy my conscience; but send me your positive command, in such full and express terms as may absolve me from all guilt and punishment, for neglecting this opportunity of doing good, when you and I shall appear before the great and awful tribunal of our LORD JESUS CHRIST.[2]

After such a convincing argument, what could Samuel Wesley say? There is no record that he ever wrote back to his wife commanding her to stop what she was doing. But, as she said in her letter, Susanna halted the meetings when Mr. Wesley returned home.

At that time, Samuel enjoyed the abundant fruit of her labors. His children had been spiritually nurtured in all the counsel of God's Word. His parish had grown in attendance and in the spiritual stature of Christ. His neighbors were now favorably disposed toward him for the first time in his ministry at Epworth.

---

[2]Clarke, 391–393.

Through Susanna's Sunday meetings, "all those persons who had been soured against Mr. Wesley for the part that he had taken in an unpopular election, now became the friends of his family; so that, to use Mrs. Wesley's own words, they lived together in the greatest amity imaginable."[3]

There were no more gunshots or loud shouting in the middle of the night in front of the Wesleys' home. The children no longer feared for their lives but played freely in the front yard. There were no more fires or destruction to their property. These spiritually rejuvenated neighbors could not have been responsible for the antics of "Old Jeffery." By the time Old Jeffery made his appearance in 1715, most of the neighboring peoples had been reconciled to the rector and his family.

It is important to point out that the impact of Susanna's Sunday meetings went far beyond the Epworth neighbors. In many respects, the content and the structure of her meetings formed the basis of the entire Methodist movement.

Adam Clarke was convinced that the seeds of Methodism were first sown in Susanna Wesley's meetings:

It is worthy of remark that Mrs. Wesley terms the people that composed these meetings, our SOCIETY; and the meetings were conducted much after the manner of the Methodist's Society meetings at this day; especially those of the sabbath evenings; when, after the preaching, the society, and often any other serious person, is permitted to stay to a second meeting, in which such exhortations are given relative to personal and family religion as could not with propriety be brought before a mixed congregation, where perhaps the bulk of the people are unawakened, and consequently incapable

---

[3]Clarke, 394.

of profiting by instructions relative to the life and power of godliness.[4]

It will never be fully known just how much good came out of Susanna's Sunday meetings. One thing is for sure, God used this remarkable woman in an extraordinary way to bring peace and reconciliation to a hostile people and a divided community.

But Susanna Wesley was still unquestionably a daughter of her era. In every way she humbly submitted to her husband's authority and recognized and accepted the limitations set on her concerning religious involvement.

Yet, at the same time, Susanna was an innovator, a woman well beyond her times. She was not afraid to be different or to tread uncharted territories; that is, if she was convinced it was the will of God.

She was not afraid to break cultural norms, even though she knew it would bring unbridled criticism. She honored the name of God and feared him more than the wrath of the people.

There came a time, however, when the attacks on Susanna and her teaching methods seemed justified. Her motives were called into question, and, as a result, her shining example of godliness and piety was severely compromised.

---

[4]Clarke, 393.

7

Conquering the Will

Within a period of twenty-one years, Susanna bore nineteen children. Many of them either died shortly after birth or only lived through the early childhood years. At least ten of them, however, lived long enough to fully benefit from their mother's many talents.

With firm conviction and utter abandonment, she gave her heart and soul to the welfare of her remaining ten children. She saw to it that they were, among other things, well-mannered, respectful, and well-educated. She did this at great personal cost.

However, in a manner so fitting her character, the mother of the Wesleys focused not on the temporary difficulties of the task but on its eternal reward. With regard to the particular task of teaching her children, Susanna made this statement:

> Though the education of so many children must create abundance of trouble, and will perpetually keep the mind employed as well as the body; yet I consider it no small honor to be entrusted with the care of so many souls. And if that trust be but managed with prudence and integrity, the harvest will abundantly recompense the toil of the seed-time; and it will be certainly no little inheritance to the future glory to stand forth at the last

day and say, 'Lord, here are the children which Thou
hast given me, of whom I have lost none by my ill example, nor by neglecting to instill into their minds, in
their early years, the principles of Thy true religion and
virtue!'[1]

Susanna Wesley began training her children at the
moment of their first breath. As newborns, she put them
on a strict feeding and sleeping regimen.

They ate at regularly scheduled intervals and were
consistently given a three-hour nap in the morning and
in the afternoon. Bedtime was always at eight o'clock.

As her children grew, Susanna Wesley became increasingly concerned about their education. Her boys
would eventually be able to go to a formal school. Nevertheless, she felt it was her duty to make sure they were
fully prepared to learn.

But even more than this, she wanted to make sure
that all of her children, including her girls, were given a
strong religious background. The only way she could assure this was to educate them herself.

So she developed an extensive and comprehensive educational program. Many of her teaching principles not
only anticipated what would be said in the future about
good education but they also demonstrated her vast
storehouse of knowledge and wisdom. However, in recent
years, Susanna Wesley's teaching methods have stirred
up controversy. They have brought her both praise and
criticism. Because of this, her educational techniques are
worthy of our full attention.

At the request of her famous son, John, Susanna
wrote to him and discussed in detail her methods of education. This oft-quoted and celebrated letter is vitally
important because it reveals to the fullest extent Susanna's philosophy on the care and education of children.

---

[1]Kirk, 163–164.

Epworth, July 24, 1732

Dear Son,

According to your desire, I have collected the principal rules I observed in educating my family; which I now send you as they occurred to my mind, and you may (if you think they can be of use to any) dispose of them in what order you please.

The children were always put into a regular method of living, in such things as they were capable of, from their birth; as in dressing, undressing, changing their linen, etc. The first quarter commonly passes in sleep.

After that, they were, if possible, laid into their cradles awake, and rocked to sleep; and so they were kept rocking, till it was time for them to awake. This was done to bring them to a regular course of sleeping; which at first was three hours in the morning, and three hours in the afternoon: afterward two hours, till they needed none at all.

When turned a year old (and some before) they were taught to fear the rod, and to cry softly; by which means they escaped abundance of correction they might otherwise have had; and that most odious noise of the crying of children was rarely heard in the house; but the family usually lived in as much quietness, as if there had not been a child among them.

As soon as they were grown pretty strong, they were confined to three meals a day. At dinner their little table and chairs were set by ours, where they could be overseen; and they were to eat and drink as much as they would; but not to call for anything.

If they wanted anything, they used to whisper to the maid which attended them, who came and spoke to me; and as soon as they could handle a knife and fork, they were set to our table. They were never to choose their meat, but always made to eat such things as were provided for the family.

Mornings they had always spoon-meat; sometimes at nights. But whatever they had, they were never permitted to eat, at those meals, of more than one thing; and of that sparingly enough. Drinking or eating between meals was never allowed unless in case of sickness; which seldom happened.

Nor were they to go to the kitchen to ask anything of the servants, when they were eating; if it was known they did, they were certainly beat, and the servants severely reprimanded.

At six, as soon as family prayers were over, they had their supper; at seven, the maid washed them; and, beginning at the youngest, she undressed and got them all to bed by eight; at which time she left them in their several rooms awake; for there was no such thing allowed in our house, as sitting by a child until it fell asleep.

They were constantly used to eat and drink what was given them that when any of them was ill, there was no difficulty in making them take the most unpleasant medicine; for they dare not refuse it, though some of them would throw it up. This I mention, to show that a person may be taught to take anything, though it be ever so much against his stomach.

In order to form the minds of children, the first thing to be done is to conquer their will, and bring them to an obedient temper. To inform the understanding is a work of time and must with children proceed by slow degrees as they are able to bear it; but the subjecting the will is a thing which must be done at once; and the sooner the better.

For by neglecting timely correction, they will contract a stubbornness and obstinacy, which is hardly ever after conquered; and never, without using such severity as would be as painful to me as to the child. In the esteem of the world they pass for kind and indulgent, whom I call cruel, parents who permit their children to get habits, which they know must be afterward broken.

Nay, some are so stupidly fond as in sport to teach their children to do things which, in a while after, they have severely beaten them for doing. Whenever a child is corrected, it must be conquered; and this will be no hard matter to do, if it be not grown headstrong by too much indulgence.

And when the will of a child is totally subdued, and it is brought to revere and stand in awe of the parents, then a great many childish follies and inadvertences may be passed by.

Some [offenses] should be overlooked and taken no notice of, and others mildly reproved; but no willful transgression ought ever be forgiven children; without chastisement less or more, as the nature and circumstances of the offense require.

I insist upon conquering the will of children very early, because this is the only strong and rational foundation of a religious education; without which both precept and example will be ineffectual.

But when this is thoroughly done, then a child is capable of being governed by the reason and piety of its parents, till its own understanding comes to maturity, and the principles of religion have taken root in the mind.

I cannot yet dismiss this subject. As self-will is the root of all sin and misery, so whatever clings fondly to this in children, insures their after-wretchedness and irreligion: whatever checks and mortifies it, promotes their future happiness and piety.

This is still more evident, if we further consider that religion is nothing else than doing the will of God and not our own; that the one grand impediment to our temporal and eternal happiness being this self-will, no indulgence of it can be trivial, no denial unprofitable.

Heaven or hell depends on this alone. So that the parent who studies to subdue his child works together with God in the renewing and saving a soul. The parent who indulges it does the devil's work, makes religion impracticable, salvation unattainable; and does all that in him lies to damn the child, soul and body forever.

The children of this family were taught, as soon as

they could speak, the Lord's Prayer, which they were made to say at rising and bedtime constantly; to which, as they grew bigger, were added a short prayer for their parents, and some Collects; a short Catechism, and some portion of Scripture, as their memories could bear.

They were very early made to distinguish the Sabbath from other days; before they could well speak or go. They were as soon taught to be still at family prayers, and to ask a blessing immediately after, which they used to do by signs, before they could kneel or speak.

They were quickly made to understand they might have nothing they cried for, and instructed to speak nicely for what they wanted. They were not to ask even the lowest servant for anything without saying, "Please give me such a thing;" and the servant was reprimanded, if she ever let them omit that word. Taking God's name in vain, cursing and swearing, profaneness, obscenity, rude, ill-bred names, were never heard among them. Nor were they ever permitted to call each other by their proper names, without the addition of brother or sister.

None of them were taught to read till five years old, except Kezzy, in whose case I was overruled; and she was more years learning than any of the rest had been months.

The way of teaching was this: The day before a child began to learn, the house was set in order, everyone's work appointed them, and a charge given, that none should come into the room from nine till twelve, or from two till five; which, you know, were our school hours.

One day was allowed the child wherein to learn its letters; great and small, except Molly and Nancy, who were a day and half before they knew them perfectly; for which I then thought them very dull; but since I have observed how long many children are learning the horn book, I have changed my opinion.

But the reason why I thought them so then was because the rest learned so readily; and your brother Samuel, who was the first child I ever taught, learned the alphabet in a few hours. He was five years old on the tenth of February; the next day he began to learn; and as soon as he knew the letters, began at the first chapter of Genesis.

He was taught to spell the first verse, then to read it over and over, till he could read it offhand without any hesitation; so on to the second, etc., till he took ten verses for a lesson, which he quickly did.

Easter fell low that year; and by Pentecost he could read a chapter very well; for he read continually, and had such a prodigious memory that I cannot remember ever to have told him the same word twice.

What was yet stranger, any word he had learned in his lesson, he knew, wherever he saw it, either in his Bible, or any other book; by which means he learned very soon to read an English author well.

The same method was observed with them all. As soon as they knew the letters, they were put first to spell, and read one line, then a verse; never leaving, till perfect in their lesson, were it shorter or longer.

So one or the other continued reading at schooltime, without any intermission; and before we left school, each child read what he had learned that morning; and before we parted in the afternoon, what they had learned all day.

There was no such thing as loud talking or playing allowed; but every one was kept close to their business for the six hours of school: And it is almost incredible what a child may be taught in a quarter of a year by a vigorous application, if it have but a tolerable capacity and good health. Every one of these, Kezzy excepted, could read better in that time than most women can do as long as they live.

Rising out of their places or going out of the room was not permitted, unless for good cause; and running into the yard, garden, or street, without leave, was always esteemed a capital offense.

For some years we went on very well. Never were children in better order. Never were children better disposed to piety, or in more subjection to their parents; till that fatal dispersion of them, after the fire, into several families.

In those they were left at full liberty to converse with servants, which before they had always been restrained from; and to run abroad, and play with any children, good or bad. They soon learned to neglect a strict observation of the Sabbath, and got knowledge of several songs and bad things, which before they had no notion of.

That civil behavior, which made them admired when at home by all that saw them, was in great measure lost; and a clownish accent and many rude ways were learned, which were not reformed without some difficulty.

When the house was rebuilt, and the children all brought home, we entered upon a strict reform; and then was begun the custom of singing psalms at the beginning and leaving of school, morning and evening.

Then also that of general retirement at five o'clock was entered upon; when the oldest took the youngest that could speak, and the second the next, to whom they read the Psalms for the day and a chapter in the New Testament; as, in the morning, they were directed to read the Psalms and a chapter in the Old: after which they went to their private prayers, before they got their breakfast, or came into the family. And I thank God, the custom is still preserved among us.

There were several by-laws observed among us, which slipped my memory, or else they had been inserted in their proper place; but I mention them here, because I think them useful.

(1) It had been observed, that cowardice and fear of punishment often lead children into lying, till they get a custom of it, which they cannot leave. To prevent this, a law was made that whoever was charged with a fault, of

which they were guilty, if they would ingenuously confess it, and promise to amend, should not be beaten.

This rule prevented a great deal of lying and would have done more, if one in the family would have observed it. But he could not be persuaded, and was therefore often accused falsely; which none would have used (except one) had they been kindly dealt with. And some, in spite of all, would always speak truth plainly.

(2) That no sinful action such as lying, stealing, playing at church or on the Lord's Day, disobedience, quarreling, etc., should ever go unpunished.

(3) That no child should ever be reprimanded or beaten twice for the same fault; and that if they amended, they should never be blamed again.

(4) That every signal act of obedience, especially when it was against their own inclinations, should be always commended, and frequently rewarded, according to the merits of the cause.

(5) That if ever any child performed an act of obedience, or did anything with an intention to please, though the performance was not well, yet the obedience and intention should be kindly accepted; and the child with sweetness directed how to do better for the future.

(6) That propriety be inviolably preserved, and none to invade the property of another in the smallest matter, though it were of little value; which they might not take from the owner, without, much less against, his consent.

This rule can never be impressed upon a child too much; and from the lack of parents and governors doing it as they should, proceeds that shameful neglect of justice which we may observe in the world.

(7) That promises be strictly observed; and a gift given should not be taken back; unless it were conditional, and the condition of the obligation not performed.

(8) That no girl be taught to work till she can read very well; and then that she be kept to her work with the same application and for the same time that she was held to reading.

This rule also is much to be observed; for the putting children to learn sewing before they can read perfectly is the very reason why so few women can read fit to be heard, and never to be well understood.

There are many commendable aspects to Susanna Wesley's teaching methods. First, from the very beginning, she regulated her children's daily schedule. This created in them a sense of security and trust that stayed with them all of their lives.

Second, she taught her children from a very early age to honor their parents. The benefits of this were far reaching. The Wesley children learned to treat all adults with proper respect. Wherever they went, they were praised for their reverent and obedient behavior.

Third, Susanna Wesley did many things that childhood experts now acknowledge to be good child-rearing and teaching methodologies. For instance, James Dobson confirms that "her beliefs reflect the traditional understanding of child-rearing."[2]

By this he means the idea of "conquering the will." Dr. Dobson agrees with Susanna Wesley that if a "child is allowed by indulgence to develop habits of defiance and disrespect during his early childhood, those characteristics will haunt him for the next twenty years."[3]

But it is at precisely this point that Susanna Wesley has come under severe criticism. She has been accused of having been too harsh and overbearing with her children. On more than one occasion, she has been portrayed as a tyrant, a mother who never let her children play or have fun.

However, we must understand Susanna according to her own times. Cruelty, especially toward children, was

[2]James Dobson, *Parenting Isn't For Cowards* (Dallas: Word Publishing, 1987), 89.
[3]Ibid., 90.

widespread. It was quite common for a child to be brutally beaten at home and at school. Youths could be subject to forced labor and then mercilessly mistreated if they failed the task.

On the other side of the spectrum, many children in Susanna's day were spoiled rotten by wealthy parents. They were neither disciplined nor taught good manners. Susanna referred to the parents of such children as being "cruel" and as doing "the devil's work."

In light of her era, Susanna's disciplinary methods were considerably mild and constructive. The Wesley children learned to "fear the rod" and obey their parents. But they were also anchored securely in their mother's love.

"Her skill and love and patience were repaid by the responsiveness and aptitude of the children. Even more, she gained their love and lasting respect. If for a time they felt they were under law, they quickly passed to the condition of being under grace. She gave them not only knowledge but a zeal for more; no merely forced obedience could have accomplished that."[4]

Susanna's teaching techniques, along with her diligence and patience, brought her much success. The Wesley children blossomed into bright and intelligent men and women. Even Samuel marveled at her work.

On one occasion, he watched her closely and said, "I wonder at your patience; you have told that child twenty times the same thing." To which she quickly commented, "If I had satisfied myself by mentioning it only nineteen times, I should have lost all my labor. It was the twentieth time that crowned it."[5]

Unlike many in our day, Susanna Wesley understood her children from a biblical perspective. Knowing that

---

[4]Edwards, 67.
[5]Ibid., 67.

they were born in sin and prone to go their own way, she brought them under submission with a firm but loving hand.

She understood that conquering the will of her children, that is, to teach them proper respect for authority, was the only way to nurture their spirits. Nothing on earth was more important to Susanna than saving the souls of her children.

8

Nurturing the Spirit

In a letter to her son John, Susanna wrote, "No one can without renouncing the world in the most literal sense observe my method: and there are few, if any, that would entirely devote above twenty years of the prime of life in hope to save the souls of their children, which they think may be saved without so much bother: for that was my principal intention, however unskillfully and unsuccessfully managed."[1]

Susanna Wesley used primarily two methods to communicate Christian truth to her children. The first was personal interaction, in which she taught her children on an individual basis and in the classroom.

The individual meetings were probably the most effective and influential means she used to achieve her goal. They had a tremendous impact on her children. John was especially impressed by them. While at Oxford University, he wrote to his mother expressing his need again for her individual attention:

> In many things you have interceded for me and prevailed. Who knows but in this too (the renunciation of the world) you may be successful? If you can spare me only that little part of Thursday evening which you for-

---

[1]Edwards, 77.

mally bestowed upon me in another manner, I doubt not it would be as useful now for correcting my heart, as it was then for forming my judgment.[2]

In the classroom, Susanna sprinkled biblical truth throughout every aspect of learning. As we observed in the previous chapter, morning, noon, and evening presented an opportunity for the children to learn about God.

Not only were the Wesley children taught to acknowledge God throughout the day, but they were constantly reminded in and out of the classroom that religion played an important role in every area of life.

Hence, their classroom education included an in-depth study of biblical principles and a serious examination of how they applied to everyday life.

The second method she used to communicate Christian truth to her children was her own written word. In a well-planned and methodical fashion, she educated them on the topics of natural revelation, divine revelation, and moral law.

She achieved this monumental task by preparing three theological manuals. In the first manual, she discussed how the order and design of creation testified to the existence of God. She argued against the idea that the universe came into existence by chance and against the assumption that matter is eternal.

As an introduction to the other two manuals, Susanna also discussed the need for divine revelation and intervention. Unfortunately, the original first manual was destroyed in the rectory fire of 1709. She did, however, manage to rewrite it in 1712.

Using the Apostle's Creed as the format in her second manual, she expounded on the great doctrines of the Christian faith. Everything from the creation to the fall

---

[2]Edwards, 68.

to the need for salvation in Christ to the future glories of heaven was written with clarity, beauty, and finesse.

In her third manual, Susanna used the Ten Commandments as a springboard to communicate to her children the major tenets of divine moral law. She taught them first and foremost that God's moral law was universal in nature, binding on all human beings for all time.

Besides these three manuals, Susanna wrote numerous letters to her children. Each of them, being as theologically instructive as the manuals, equally showed forth her rare and unusual talents.

In fact, her exposition on the Apostle's Creed was actually a letter written to her daughter Sukey while she was living with her Uncle Matthew in London. Sukey and her sister Hetty, you will remember, went to live with him after the Epworth fire of 1709.

This letter reveals Susanna's vast knowledge of theological truth and her understanding of the salvation message. For this reason, it is important to understand the ebb and flow of her explanations in her own words.

The first part of her letter is an introduction to the several major Bible doctrines. Susanna wrote such a detailed and complex introduction that many have questioned the need for her to even expound on the Apostle's Creed.

However, keeping in mind that this letter was intended to be an instructive manual for all of her children, she gave a full account of the Apostle's Creed in order to help them understand the systematic development of Christian truth.

Epworth, January 13, 1710
Dear Sukey,

Since our misfortunes have separated us from each other, and we can no longer enjoy the opportunities we once had of conversing together, I can no other way discharge the duty of a parent, or comply with my inclination of doing you all the good I can, but by writing.

You know very well how I love you. I love your body; and do earnestly beseech almighty God to bless it with health, and all things necessary for its comfort and support in this world. But my tenderest regard is for your immortal soul, and for its spiritual happiness; which regard I cannot better express, than by endeavoring to instill into your mind those principles of knowledge and virtue that are absolutely necessary in order to your leading a good life here, which is the only thing that can infallibly secure your happiness hereafter.

The main thing which is now to be done is to lay a good foundation, that you may act upon principles and be always able to satisfy yourself and give a reason to others of the faith that is in you: for any one who makes a profession of religion, only because it is the custom of the country in which they live, or because their parents do so, or their worldly interest is thereby secured or advanced, will never be able to stand in the day of temptation; nor shall they ever enter into the kingdom of heaven.

And though, perhaps, you cannot at present comprehend all I shall say, yet keep this letter by you, and as you grow in years your reason and judgment will improve and you will obtain a more clear understanding in all things.

You have already been instructed in some of the first principles of religion: that there is one, and but one God; that in the unity of the Godhead there are three distinct persons, Father, Son, and Holy Ghost; that this God ought to be worshiped. You have learned some prayers, your creed, and catechism, in which is briefly comprehended your duty to God, yourself, and your neighbor.

But, Sukey, it is not learning these things by heart, nor your saying a few prayers morning and night, that will bring you to heaven; you must understand what you say, and you must practice what you know: and since knowledge is requisite in order to practice, I shall endeavor (after as plain a manner as I can) to instruct you in some of those fundamental points which are most necessary to be known, and most easy to be understood. And I earnestly beseech the great Father of spirits to guide your mind into the way of truth.

Though it has been generally acknowledged that the being and perfection of God, and a great part of man's duty toward him, is that we should love him, and pray to him for what we want, and praise him for what we enjoy, as likewise much of our duty toward ourselves and neighbor are discoverable by the light of nature, that is, by that understanding and reason which are natural to man; yet considering the present state of mankind, it was absolutely necessary that we should have some revelation from God to make known to us those truths upon the knowledge of which our salvation depends, and which, unassisted, reason could never have discovered.

For all the duties of natural religion, and all the hopes of happiness that result from the performance of them, are all concluded within the present life; nor could we have had any certainty of the FUTURE STATE of the being of SPIRITS, of the immortality of the soul, or of a judgment to come.

And though we may perceive that all men have by nature a strong bent or bias toward evil and a great averseness from God and goodness; that our understandings, wills, and affections, etc., are extremely corrupted and depraved; yet how could we have known by what means we became so, or how sin and death entered into the world?

Since we are assured that whatever is absolutely perfect, as God is, could never be the author of evil; and we are as sure that whatever is corrupt or impure must necessarily be offensive and displeasing to the most holy God, there is nothing more opposite than good and evil.

Nay, further, sin is not only displeasing to God, as it

is contrary to the purity of his divine nature, but it is the highest affront and indignity to his sacred majesty imaginable.

By it his most wise and holy laws are condemned and violated, and his honor most impiously treated; and therefore he is in justice obliged to punish such contempt, and to vindicate the honor of his own laws: nor can he, without detracting from his infinite perfection, pardon such offenders, or remit the punishment they deserve, without full satisfaction made to his justice.

Now I would gladly know which way his justice could be satisfied, since it is impossible for a finite being like man to do it; or how the nature of man should be renewed, or he again be admitted into the favor of God; or how reason could suggest that our weak endeavors and petitions should be acceptable instead of perfect obedience, unless some other were substituted in our stead that would undergo the punishment we have deserved and thereby satisfy divine justice and purchase pardon and favor with God, the merit of whose perfect obedience should atone for the imperfection of ours, and so obtain for us a title to those glorious rewards, to that eternal happiness, of which we must acknowledge ourselves utterly unworthy and of which we must have despaired without such a Savior?

Or how should we have had any certainty of our salvation, unless God had revealed these things to us? The soul is immortal, and must survive all time, even to eternity; and consequently it must have been miserable to the utmost extent of its duration, had we not had that sacred treasure of knowledge which is contained in the books of the Old and New Testaments. A treasure infinitely more valuable than the whole world, because therein we find all things necessary for our salvation.

There also we find many truths, which, though we cannot say it is absolutely necessary that we should know them, (since it is possible to be saved without that knowledge), yet it is highly convenient that we should, because they give us great light into those things that are necessary to be known, and solve many doubts that could not otherwise be cleared.

Thus we collect from many passages of Scripture, that before God created the visible world, or ever he made man, he created a higher rank of intellectual beings, which we call angels or spirits; and these were those bright morning stars mentioned in Job, which sung together; those sons of God that shouted for joy when the foundations of the earth were laid.

To these he gave a law or rule of action, as he did afterward to the rest of his creation; and they being free agents, having a principle of liberty, of choosing or refusing, and of acting accordingly, as they must have, or they could not properly be called either good or evil; for upon this principle of freedom or liberty the principle of election or choice is founded; and upon the choosing good or evil depends the being virtuous or vicious, since liberty is the formal essence of moral virtue; that is, it is the free choice of a rational being that makes them either good or bad; nor could any one that acts by necessity be ever capable of rewards or punishments; the angels, I say, being free agents, must, I think, necessarily be put on some trial of their obedience; and so consequently were at first only placed in a state of probation or trial.

Those who made a good use of their liberty, and chose to obey the law of their Creator, and acquiesced in the order of the divine wisdom, which had disposed them in several ranks and orders subservient to each other, were, by the almighty decree, confirmed in their state of blessedness; nor are they now capable of any defection.

But those accursed spirits that rebelled against their Maker, and aspired above the rank in which his providence had placed them, were, for their presumption, justly excluded from the celestial paradise, and condemned to perpetual torments, which were the necessary consequences of their apostasy.

After the fall of the angels, and perhaps to supply

their defects, it pleased the eternal Goodness to create Adam, who was the first general head of mankind; and in him was virtually included the whole species of human nature.

He was somewhat inferior to the angels, being composed of two different natures, body and soul. The former was material, or matter made of the earth; the latter immaterial, or a spiritual substance, created after the image of God.

And as man was also a rational free agent like the angels, so it was agreeable to the eternal Wisdom to place him likewise in a state of probation; and the trial of his obedience was not eating of the tree of the knowledge of good and evil, and the penalty of his disobedience was death.

This trial was suited to the double or mixed nature of man; the beauty, scent, and taste of the fruit was the trial of their senses or appetites; and the virtue of it being not only good for food but also to be desired to make one wise, was the trial of their minds; and by this God made proof of our first parents, to see whether they would deny their sensual appetites, and keep the body in subjection to the mind; or whether they would prefer the pleasures of sense, and thereby dethrone their reason, break the covenant of their obedience, and forfeit the favor of God and eternal happiness; and whether they would humbly be content with that measure of knowledge and understanding which God thought best for them, or boldly pry into those things which he had forbidden them to search after.

Now the devil, envying the happiness of our first parents, being grieved that any less perfect beings should possess the place he had lost, took occasion from the reasonable trial God had proposed to Adam, to attack the woman by a subtle question, "Has God really said that you shall not eat of every tree of the garden?

"Has he created this beautiful world, this great variety of creatures, for your use and enjoyment, and made these delicious fruits which he himself has pronounced good, and yet forbidden you to taste them?"

To which she replied, "We may eat of the fruit of the trees of the garden; but of the fruit of the tree in the middle of the garden, God has said, you shall not eat of it, neither shall you touch it, lest you die."

Upon which the malicious tempter boldly presumed to give the lie to his Maker: "You shall not surely die; for God does know that in the day you eat of it, then your eyes shall be opened, and you shall be as gods, knowing good and evil."

And when the woman saw that the tree was good for food, and that it was pleasant to the eyes, and a tree to be desired to make one wise, she took of the fruit and ate it, and gave also to her husband with her, and he ate it, etc.

Thus pride and sensuality ruined our first parents, and brought them and their posterity into a state of mortality. Thus sin entered into the world, and death by sin, and thus was human nature corrupted at its foundation; and as a corrupt tree cannot bring forth good fruit, so of consequence the children of guilty Adam must be corrupt and depraved.

Anyone who will make the least reflection on his own mind, may soon be convinced of this great truth, that not only the body is weak and infirm, subject to many diseases, liable to many ill accidents, and even to death itself, but also the superior powers of the soul are weakened; as the apostle expresses it, "at enmity with God."

The understanding, which was designed chiefly to be exercised in the knowledge and contemplation of the supreme Being, is darkened; nor can it, without the divine assistance, discern the radiant glories of the Deity. And though it should naturally press after truth, as being its proper object; yet it seldom, and not without great difficulty, attains to the knowledge of it; but it is subject to ignorance, which is the sin of the understanding, because it generally proceeds from our natural indisposition to search after truth.

Error is the sin or defect of the judgment, mistaking one thing for another, not having clear and distinct apprehensions of things; for which reason it is frequently guilty of making wrong determinations. Not choosing or not inclining to good, or adhering to and preferring evil before it, is the sin of the will.

A readiness in receiving vain, impure, corrupt ideas or images, and a backwardness in receiving good and useful ideas, is the sin of the imagination or fancy; and a facility in retaining evil and vain ideas, and a neglect of or a readiness to let slip those which are good, is the sin or defect of the memory.

Loving, hating, desiring, fearing, etc., what we should not love, hate, desire, fear, etc., at all in the least degree; or when the object of such passions are lawful, to love, hate desire, etc., more than reason requires; or else not loving, hating, desiring, etc., when we ought to love, hate, desire, etc.; in short, any error, either in defect or excess, either too much or too little, is the vice or sin of the passions or affections of the soul.

Now, if we consider the infinite, boundless, incomprehensible perfection of the ever-blessed God, we may easily conceive that evil, that sin is the greatest contradiction imaginable to his most holy nature; and that no evil, no disease, pain, or natural uncleanness whatever, is so hateful, so loathsome to us, as the corruption and imperfection of the soul is to him.

He is infinite purity, absolutely separated from all moral imperfection. The divine intellect is all brightness, all perfect; was never, and can never be capable of the least ignorance. He is TRUTH; nor can he be weary or indisposed in contemplating that great attribute of his most perfect nature, but has a constant, steady view of truth.

And as he fully comprehends at once all things past, present, and to come; so all objects appear to him simple, naked, undisguised in their natures, properties, relations, and ends, truly as they are; nor is it possible that he should be guilty of error or mistake; or making any false judgment or wrong determination.

He is goodness, and his most holy will cannot swerve or decline from what is so. He always wills what is absolutely best; nor can he possibly be deceived or deceive anyone.

The ideas of the divine Mind are amiable, clear, holy, just, good, useful; and he is of purer eyes than to behold iniquity. His love, desire, etc., though boundless, immense, and infinite, are yet regular, immutable, always under the direction of his unerring wisdom, his unlimited goodness, and his impartial justice.

But who can by searching find out God? Who can find out the Almighty to perfection? What angel is worthy to speak his praise, who dwells in the inaccessible light which no man can approach?

And though he is always surrounded by thousands and tens of thousands of those pure and happy spirits, yet they are represented to us as veiling their faces, as if conscious of too much imperfection and weakness to behold his glory. And if he charged his angels with folly, and the stars are not pure in his sight, how much less man, that is a worm; and the son of man, that is a worm?

And as we are thus corrupt and impure by nature, so are we likewise the children of wrath, and in a state of damnation; for it was not only a temporal death with which God threatened our first parents, if they were disobedient; but it was also a spiritual death, an eternal separation from him who is our life; the consequence of which separation is our eternal misery.

But the infinite goodness of God, who delights that his mercy should triumph over justice, though he provided no remedy for the fallen angels, yet man being a more simple kind of creature, who perhaps did not sin so maliciously against so much knowledge as those apostate spirits did, he would not subject the whole race of mankind to be ruined and destroyed by the fraud and subtlety of Satan; but he gave us help by one who was mighty, that is able and willing to save to the uttermost all such as shall come to God through him.

And this Savior was that seed of the woman that was promised should bruise the head of the serpent, break the power of the devil, and bring mankind again into a savable condition. And upon a view of that satisfaction which Christ would make for the sins of the whole world was the penalty of Adam's disobedience suspended, and he submitted to a second trial; and God renewed his covenant with man, not on the former condition of perfect obedience, but on condition of faith in Christ Jesus, and a sincere though imperfect obedience of the laws of God. I will speak something of these two branches of our duty distinctly.

By faith in Christ is to be understood an assent to whatever is recorded of him in Holy Scripture; or is said to be delivered by him, either immediately by himself, or mediately by his prophets and apostles; or whatever may, by just inferences or natural consequences, be collected from their writings.

But because the greater part of mankind either want leisure or capacity to collect the several articles of faith which lie scattered up and down throughout the sacred writ, the wisdom of the Church has thought fit to sum them up in a short form of words, commonly called THE APOSTLE'S CREED, which, because it comprehends the main of what a Christian ought to believe, I shall briefly explain to you.

And though I have not time at present to bring all the arguments I could to prove the being of God, his divine attributes, and the truth of revealed religion; yet this short paraphrase may inform you what you should intend when you make the solemn confession of our most holy faith; and may teach you that it is not to be said after a formal, customary manner, but seriously, as in the presence of the almighty God, who observes whether the heart join with the tongue, and whether your mind

do truly assent to what you profess, when you say. . . .[3]
(See Appendix 1 for the actual exposition of the Creed.)

This remarkable introduction in her letter to Sukey not only reveals Susanna Wesley's incredible mental capacities, but it also provides some insight into the interpretation of Scripture in her day.

At every point, the major themes of the Bible were understood by her according to orthodox tradition. This means the letter reflects to some degree that the Established Church, to which Susanna belonged, still embraced the faith that was passed on by the apostles of Jesus.

Her focus on reason and the intellect also mirrors the day in which she lived. The Age of Reason was in full swing at that time. Her systematic representation of truth in light of human reason and judgment was the typical way of expressing such topics in her day.

Susanna was also well acquainted with many of the writings of the leading philosophers of her day, including John Locke. While she was clearly influenced by their rational ideas, they did not taint her orthodox beliefs.

But this letter, more than anything else, gives us a glimpse into the mind and heart of Susanna Wesley. It reveals her ardent zeal to educate her children in every aspect of biblical truth.

Her passion for the souls of her children cannot be denied. Their spiritual welfare consumed her and occupied her every waking moment.

A portion of a letter to her eldest son, Samuel, further illuminates the yearnings of this mother's heart for the souls of her children:

> I exhort you, as I am your faithful friend; and I command you, as I am your parent, to use your utmost dil-

---

[3]Clark, 347–354.

igence to make your calling and election sure; to be faithful to your God; and after I have said that, I need not bid you be industrious in your calling. . . . I have a great and just desire that all your sisters and your brothers should be saved as well as you. . . .

I weep and pray in my retirements from the world, when no mortal knows the agonies of my soul upon your account, no eye sees my tears, which are only beheld by that Father of spirits, of whom I so urgently beg grace for you, that I hope I may at last be heard! Is it possible that you should be damned? Oh, that it were impossible! Indeed, I think I could almost wish myself accursed, so I were sure of your salvation.[4]

Susanna's vigorous teaching methods and earnest prayers were undoubtedly a great benefit to her children. But were they responsive to their mother's teachings and example?

In 1735 Charles asked John to accompany him on a trip to America. John went with the outward goal of evangelizing the heathen. But his journal reveals his inward motives were quite different.

John's true purpose for going was "the hope of saving my own soul. I hope to learn the true sense of the Gospel by preaching it to the heathen. . . . I went to America to convert the Indians but, oh, who shall convert me?"

---

[4]Kirk, 159.

9

The Mother of Methodism

Early in the eighteenth century, England began to experience a moral decline. There were two major factors that attributed to this downfall: the rise of deism and the apathy of clergymen.

The upper classes were the first to embrace the rationalistic religion of deism. The deists held that God was the First Cause of creation. But then he withdrew his hand and allowed his creation to function under natural laws.

The deists also argued that there was no place in the natural order for supernatural intervention. They did not believe in the miracles of the Bible or in the Incarnation of Jesus or in the need to be cleansed from sin.

Human reason was held supreme by the deists. God was indeed to be worshiped but only by means of living a moral life, which they believed could be accomplished without divine aid. The Bible was considered to be only a code of ethics.

As deism increased in popularity, the influence of the high clergymen over the common people decreased. For the most part, they were apathetic and unfeeling. Their sermons were "often only long homilies filled with moral platitudes."[1]

---

[1]Cairns, 382.

"The Anglican Church had become an ecclesiastical system, under which the people of England had lapsed into heathenism, or a state hardly to be distinguished from it."[2]

Someone who had visited the country in 1730 wrote, "There is no such thing as religion in England; if any one speaks about religion everybody begins to laugh." Gambling and drinking were widespread.

In fact, the death rate skyrocketed in the early part of the century because of the massive consumption of cheap gin. This was the sad state of England at this stage in history; that is, until the rise of Methodism.

Methodism made a profound impact on English society. It utterly transformed the spiritual and moral condition of the people. It was also largely responsible for England's role as the great peacekeeper of the world during the tumultuous nineteenth century.

Much of the success of the entire Methodist movement can be traced back directly to its founder, John Wesley. He strongly believed that the gospel message was intended to impact a society. So he vehemently opposed social evils such as drunkenness and slavery.

"This neat, almost dapper, little hardworking man had under God transformed the religious life of the workers of England."[3] Because of Wesley, gin trafficking in England came to a halt and the public attitude toward slavery began to change.

In 1746 he founded the first free medical dispensary in England. Much of his ministry was spent visiting the sick, giving to the needy, and preaching to the masses in the open fields.

Speaking of his ministry, Mr. Wesley said, "I look upon the world as my parish." But the founder of Meth-

---

[2]Kirk, 274.
[3]Cairns, 384.

odism did not always have this compassionate world-view. During his teens and twenties, he described himself as being "cold and indifferent" toward both God and people.

John's journey to spiritual peace was a long and difficult one. But his mother was a continual source of encouragement. Long before John's life-changing experience on Aldersgate Street, which sparked the Methodist movement, Susanna was shaping his views and guiding his steps.

It was said of her, however, that she lived long enough to "deplore the extravagances of her sons." Is there any truth to this claim? Because of the decisive role Susanna played in the development of Methodism, it is important to thoroughly explore this touchy issue.

But first, it is crucial to understand the progression of influence Susanna had in John's personal life. Her counsel, along with his conversion experience and God's leading, inspired him to develop one of the most fruitful Christian ministries the world has ever seen.

In 1728, while at Oxford University, John's younger brother, Charles, experienced a spiritual awakening. He became fervent in prayer and spent much of his time visiting the poor and the sick. He gathered around him other like-minded students and formed the Holy Club, which later became known as the Methodist Society.

Though he still had no peace in his soul, John also became a member of this group. Eventually he even assumed leadership. As was his usual practice, John informed his mother about the group and their activities.

To which she replied, "I heartily join with your small society in all their pious and charitable actions, which are intended for God's glory. . . . May you still in such good works go on and prosper!"[4]

---

[4]Clark, 396.

During his early years at Oxford, John had frequently consulted his mother on some difficult theological questions. One of them had to do with the doctrine of predestination.

He wrote to her and expressed his concerns about the matter. John believed that the strict Calvinistic view, which taught the total depravity of human beings and the divine predestination of some to be damned and some to be saved, was against reason and contrary to scriptural teachings.

Susanna agreed with his views and, in the following letter, communicated her thoughts on the subject. The outcome of this exchange between mother and son was extremely significant. John ultimately adopted her view and incorporated it into his form of Methodism.

July 18, 1725
Dear Son,

I have often wondered that men should be so vain to amuse themselves by searching into the decrees of God, which no human wit can fathom; and do not rather employ their time and powers in working out their salvation, and making their own calling and election sure.

Such studies tend more to confound than to inform the understanding; and young people had best let them alone. But since I find you have some scruples concerning our article of predestination, [Article No. 17 in the Anglican Articles of Religion] I will tell you my thoughts on the matter, and if they satisfy not, you may desire your father's direction, who is surely better qualified than me.

The doctrine of predestination as maintained by rigid Calvinists is very shocking, and ought to be abhorred because it charges the most holy God with being the author of sin. And I think you reason very well and justly against it; for it is certainly inconsistent with the justice and goodness of God to lay man under either a physical or moral necessity of committing sin, and then punish him for doing it. Far be this from the Lord! Shall not the Judge of all the earth do right!

I do firmly believe that God, from all eternity, has elected some to everlasting life; but then I humbly conceive that this election is founded in his foreknowledge, according to that in the eighth of Romans, verses 29–30: "Whom he did foreknow, he also did predestinate to be conformed to the image of his Son. . . . Moreover, whom he did predestinate, them he also called: and whom he called, them he also justified: and whom he justified, them he also glorified."

Whom, in his eternal prescience, God saw would make a right use of their powers, and accept of offered mercy, he did predestinate, adopt for his children, his peculiar treasure. And that they might be conformed to the image of his only Son, he called them to himself by his eternal Word, through the preaching of the gospel; and internally by his Holy Spirit: which call they obeying, repenting of their sins, and believing in the Lord Jesus, he justifies them, absolves them from the guilt of all their sins, and acknowledges them as just and righteous persons, through the merits and mediation of Jesus Christ. And having thus justified, he receives them to glory, to heaven.

This is the sum of what I believe concerning predestination, which I think is agreeable to the analogy of faith; since it does in no wise detract from the glory of God's free grace, nor impair the liberty of man. Nor can it with more reason be supposed that the prescience of God is the cause that so many finally perish, than our knowing the sun will rise tomorrow is the cause of its rising.[5]

It is a well-known fact that John Wesley was responsible for the revival of Arminianism in evangelical Chris-

---

[5]Kline, 21–22.

tianity. This letter serves to show that the source of his teachings on this subject was his mother.

Even in his preaching style Susanna's sway could be detected. Similar to her own straightforward teaching style, John's approach was simple, direct, and free from "unnecessary niceties."

Those Sunday meetings that Susanna held in the rectory kitchen during John's boyhood made such a profound impression on him that he modeled them in his Methodist societies. His Methodist meetings mimicked her Sunday meetings both in content and structure.

John even referred to his mother's Sunday meetings at her funeral saying, "I cannot but further observe, that even she, as well as her father, and grandfather, her husband, and her three sons, had been, in her measure and degree, a preacher of righteousness!"[6]

Susanna's innovative and unconventional methods carried over into John's life and ministry in the most extraordinary ways. But none was more significant for Methodism than the concept of lay preaching.

There came a time in John's fruitful ministry when the Church of England, for which he was an ordained minister, excluded him from participating in the services and Sacraments. Both he and his followers were expelled because they were considered fanatics and zealots.

John then took his ministry to the open fields and the marketplaces in London to preach to everyone who would listen. Many people came to Christ during that time. He divided them into small societies and bands, which were spread throughout the London district.

The time soon came for John to move on and preach the gospel elsewhere, but he was deeply concerned for the welfare of his London societies. Since the Church of

---

[6]Kirk, 297.

England had turned him out, there was no one to care for them.

So he appointed Thomas Maxwell, an unordained yet capable leader, to take care of these London societies. Maxwell was to meet with each band on a regular basis to encourage them and instruct them in the Scriptures.

Soon, Maxwell's reputation as a good speaker and teacher spread throughout the community. Because of the demand of the people, he was compelled to take a passage of Scripture and preach on it in the usual manner. But this procedure was highly unacceptable because Thomas Maxwell was not an ordained minister.

When John caught wind of his activities, he became deeply agitated. He quickly returned to London to stop Maxwell from shaming himself any further. When he came to the meetingplace, he was first met by his mother.

Susanna Wesley asked her son why he was so anxious. "Thomas Maxwell has turned preacher, I find," quipped John.[7] To which she hastily replied, "John, you know what my sentiments have been. You cannot suspect me of favoring readily anything of this kind.

"But take care what you do with respect to that young man; for he is as surely called of God to preach as you are. Examine what have been the fruits of his preaching, and hear him yourself."[8]

Susanna, being of High Church principles herself, knew that lay preaching was highly unconventional. But, having been raised in a nonconformist home, she also knew that God could not be limited by human tradition. She had sensed the power of God in this "unordained" preacher.

Once again, John yielded to his mother's advice and listened to Maxwell preach a sermon. Afterward, John

[7]Edwards, 81.
[8]Ibid., 81–82.

announced, "It is the Lord! Let Him do what seemeth Him good. What am I that I should withstand God?"[9]

It is clear, therefore, that Susanna Wesley was the first to support the concept of lay preaching. How significant was this to her son and to the Methodist movement? "Without lay preaching Methodism could not have become a world church, and it would have lacked what became its most distinctive element.

"Susanna argued better than she knew, for on her words great issues hung. It was one last service she rendered her son and her final contribution to the Revival whose beginnings she lived long enough to see."[10]

After all we have seen of Susanna's support of her son and her incredible influence on his doctrinal views, it was still said that she "lived long enough to deplore the extravagances of her sons John and Charles. She considered them as under strong delusion to believe a lie."[11]

A couple of events took place that caused this vicious rumor to be spread: Charles' and John's personal conversion experience and their initial ministry tactics, and a misunderstanding between them and their older brother, Samuel.

The month of May 1738 was unquestionably a defining season in church history. On May 21, Charles passed through a life-changing experience: the realization of the assurance of his salvation. Three days later, on May 24, after meeting with the same Moravian society, John went through a similar experience.

"I felt my heart strangely warmed," said John. "I felt I did trust in Christ, Christ alone for salvation; and an assurance was given me that he had taken away my sins, even mine, and saved me from the law of sin and death.[12]

---

[9]Ibid., 82.
[10]Ibid., 82.
[11]Clark, 399–400.
[12]*John Wesley's Journal*, extracts from May 24, 1738.

Being anxious to tell his mother about this life-changing experience, John read to her a paper that contained the entire account, including all his agonizing struggles for spiritual rest. She heartily approved of the experience and rejoiced in his newfound assurance.

But then something took place that caused Susanna to become alarmed at both John's and Charles' conduct. John described the event with these words:

> In the morning I came to London; and after receiving the Holy Communion at Islington, I had once more an opportunity of seeing my mother, whom I had not seen since my return from Germany. I cannot but mention an odd circumstance here. I had read her a paper in June last year, containing a short account of what had passed in my own soul, till within a few days of that time.
>
> She greatly approved it, and said she heartily blessed God, who had brought me to so just a way of thinking. While I was in Germany, a copy of that paper was sent, without my knowledge, to one of my relations. He sent an account of it to my mother; whom I now found under strange fears concerning me, being convinced, "by an account taken from one of my own papers, that I had greatly erred from the faith."
>
> I could not conceive what paper that could be; but on inquiry, found it was the same I had read her myself. How hard is it to form a true judgment of any person or thing from the account of a prejudiced relative! Yea though he be ever so honest a man: for he who gave this report was one of unquestionable veracity. And yet by his sincere account of a writing that lay before his eyes, was the truth so totally disguised that my Mother knew not the paper she had heard from end to end, nor I that I had myself wrote it.[13]

This "relation" of whom John spoke was none other

[13]Kirk, 290.

than his older brother, Samuel Wesley of Tiverton. Apparently, Mrs. Hutton, a so-called "friend" of John and Charles, sent the paper to Samuel.

Along with the paper, she wrote a fierce letter accusing the brothers of behaving fanatically and of teaching false doctrine. She claimed they taught that God assured believers of their salvation through dreams and visions.

Samuel then wrote to his mother and reported all the things he had learned about his brothers' conduct. Susanna was undoubtedly alarmed by this slanderous report about her sons. But there was no truth to his claims.

His mind had clearly been poisoned by Mrs. Hutton's letter. But long before he received her report, he was prejudiced against John and Charles. He did not approve of their highly unconventional methods of ministry.

Samuel's letter to his mother twisted the truth about John's and Charles' teachings and the nature of their ministry. Susanna then wrote back to Samuel, expressing her views and concerns.

The content of this letter has often been used to "prove" that Susanna believed the awful things Samuel said about his brothers.

However, the following short excerpt from this infamous letter will clearly show that Susanna did not speak out against her sons but against such beliefs in general:

Dear Son,

Your double letters came safe to me last Friday. I thank you for them, and have received much satisfaction in reading them. They are written with good spirit and judgment, sufficient, I should think, to satisfy any unprejudiced mind that the reviving of these pretensions to dreams, visions, etc., is not only vain and frivolous as to the matter of them but also of dangerous consequence to the weaker sort of Christian.

You have well observed "that it is not the method of Providence to use extraordinary means to bring about that for which ordinary [means] are sufficient." There-fore, the very end for which they pretend that these new revelations are sent seems to me one of the best argu-ments against the truth of them.

As far as I can see, they plead that these visions, etc., are given to assure some particular persons of their adoption and salvation. But this end is abundantly pro-vided for in the Holy Scriptures, wherein all may find the rules by which we must live here and be judged here-after so plainly laid down, "that he who runs may read;" and it is by these laws we should examine ourselves, which is a way of God's appointment, and therefore we may hope for his direction and assistance in such ex-amination.

And if, upon a serious review of our state, we find that in the tenor of our lives we have or do now sincerely desire and endeavor to perform the conditions of the gos-pel covenant required on our parts, then we may discern that the Holy Spirit has laid in our minds a good foun-dation of a strong, reasonable, and lively hope of God's mercy through Christ.[14]

This letter is far from condemning her sons' behavior. In fact, in the same context, Susanna states that George Whitefield assured her that her sons were on the right track:

He came here to see me, and we talked about your brothers. I told him I did not like their way of living, wished them in some place of their own, wherein they might regularly preach, etc. He replied, I could not con-ceive the good they did in London; that the greatest part of our clergy were asleep, and that there never was a greater need of itinerant preachers than now. Upon which a gentleman that came with him said that my son

---

[14]Clark, 401.

Charles had converted him, and that my sons spent all their time in doing good.[15]

While it is true that she had some questions about her sons' activities, she ultimately came to believe they were doing good. Indeed, Susanna could not condemn the Methodism which she, in many respects, helped to found.

Furthermore, Whitefield confirmed Susanna's support to John. In a letter to him, he wrote, "Your prayer is heard! This morning I visited your mother, whose prejudices are entirely removed, and she longs to be with you in your Societies at London. Arguments from [Samuel] in Tiverton, I believe, will now have but little weight."[16]

And, after speaking to John and Charles personally, Susanna was "thoroughly convinced they were in no delusion, but spoke the words of truth and soberness."[17]

This is truly a happy ending to this whole incident. However, a most unfortunate turn of events came as a result of John's and Charles' ministry. They were no longer "thoroughly convinced" that their mother was a true believer.

---

[15]Ibid., 402.
[16]Kirk, 292.
[17]Clark, 400.

10

Susanna's Last Years

In the latter years of his life, Susanna's husband, Samuel, was plagued with a multitude of physical problems. In 1726, at the age of sixty-four, he suffered a partial stroke, which left his right hand paralyzed.

Two years later he had two major accidents: one in a boat and one on his horse. He escaped the mishaps without severe injuries, but because of his age they took a toll on his body from which he never fully recovered.

At sixty-eight, he was involved in yet another serious accident with his wagon. This one nearly took his life. Being incapacitated for several weeks, he began to think about who would take care of Susanna in the event of his death.

He had no savings, no possessions, and was still in considerable debt. He knew Susanna would not be able to stay on at Epworth unless one of his sons succeeded him. So in 1733 Samuel wrote to his eldest son and asked him to take his place.

When Samuel Jr. declined the offer, he wrote to John, asking him if he would consider the position. Heavily involved in the Holy Club at Oxford at that time, John also turned it down.

Needless to say, both Samuel and Susanna were quite disappointed at their sons' refusal to take their father's place. At the same time, they accepted their decisions and remained in close contact with them.

In 1734, at seventy-three years of age, Samuel suffered another severe physical setback and was confined to the rectory for six months.

Unable to care for himself or to perform any of his ministerial duties, he became more and more dependent upon Susanna. In his feeble condition, Samuel wrote to John a second time in an attempt to persuade him to change his mind.

Susanna also wrote to John at this time to confirm Samuel's condition: "Your father is in a very bad state of health; he sleeps little and eats less. He seems not to have any apprehension of his approaching exit, but I fear he has but a short time to live."[1]

John finally gave in to his parents' wishes and applied for the Epworth rectorship. He even called on an influential friend to help him land the position. But he was ultimately turned down because of his unbecoming "strictness of life."

In April 1735 Samuel lay on the verge of death. Susanna wrote to John and Charles urging them to come quickly. On April 25, with his wife and four of his children gathered around him, Samuel Wesley died.

Susanna took his death very hard. But it seems that his final passing was not as difficult for her as were the few days before his death.

Charles wrote, "My mother, who for several days before he died hardly ever went into his chamber but she was carried out again in a fit, was far less shocked than we expected; and told us that "now she was heard, in his having so easy a death, and her being strengthened to bear it."[2]

---

[1]Dallimore, 151.
[2]Ibid., 155.

Unfortunately, Samuel's fears for Susanna after his death were well-founded. After his debts were paid, there was nothing left for her to live on. She became completely dependent upon the goodness of her children for her welfare.

The first one to take her in was her daughter Emilia. She was running a girls' boarding school in Gainsborough at the time and had a little room available. While she did not have the best accommodations, Emilia made her mother as comfortable as possible.

After spending about a year with her daughter, Susanna went to live with her son Samuel at Tiverton. Being married but having no children, he had plenty of room for her. He also made a good salary as a teacher, which enabled him to comfortably provide for her.

Nevertheless, in 1737, after living only a year with Samuel, Susanna moved in with her daughter Martha and her husband in Salisbury. While there, John and Charles had their conversion experiences and began their preaching ministries in London.

It was also while living with Martha that Susanna experienced a great loss. On November 5, 1739, her beloved son Samuel died suddenly and unexpectedly. Susanna deeply mourned his passing but did not despair.

In a letter to Charles, she confessed that her son's death drew her closer to the Lord:

> Your brother was exceedingly dear to me in his life, and perhaps I have erred in loving him too well. I once thought it impossible for me to bear his loss, but none know what they can bear till they are tried. . . .
>
> I rejoice in having a comfortable hope of my dear son's salvation. He is now at rest and would not return to earth to gain the world. Why then should I mourn? . . .
>
> It was natural to think that I should be troubled for my dear son's death because a considerable part of my support was cut off. But to say the truth, I have never

had one anxious thought of such matters: for it came immediately into my mind that God, by my child's loss, had called me to a firmer dependence upon himself. . . .[3]

Shortly after she wrote this letter, Susanna went to live with her son John in London. He had recently purchased the Foundry, a former factory, in which to hold his meetings. She lived out the rest of her days in his little apartment at the Foundry.

John was well able to care for his mother and to give her all the necessary comforts. She was also able to fully participate in his ministry. Shortly after coming to live with him, an important event took place in Susanna's life.

In January 1740, during a Communion service held by her son-in-law Westley Hall, Susanna realized, in a deeply personal way, that her sins were forgiven. She confessed in one of her letters:

While my son Hall was pronouncing these words in delivering the cup to me, "The blood of our Lord Jesus Christ which was given for thee," these words struck through my heart, and I knew that God for Christ's sake had forgiven me all my sins.[4]

Charles was convinced that his mother had not been truly converted until this point. In fact, he wrote to her claiming that all her previous years were spent in seeking a salvation by works.

Susanna's reply was most gracious and revealing. She did not share her son's sentiments about her spiritual condition. While she freely admitted she had "defected" from the faith for a time, she also insisted she had known Christ for many years.

I thank you for your kind letter. I call it so, because

[3]Ibid., 116–162.
[4]Ibid., 162.

I verily believe it was dictated by a sincere desire for my spiritual and eternal good. There is too much truth in many of your accusations; nor do I intend to say one word in my own defense, but rather choose to refer all things to him that knoweth all things. . . .

I am not one of those who have never been enlightened or made partaker of the heavenly gift or of the Holy Ghost, but have for many years been fully awakened, and am deeply conscious of sin, both original and actual. My case is rather like that of the Church of Ephesus; I have not been faithful to the talents committed to my trust, and have lost my first love. . . .

I do not, I will not, despair; for ever since my sad defection, when I was almost without hope, when I had forgotten God, yet I found he had not forgotten me. Even then he did by his Spirit apply the merits of the great Atonement to my soul, by telling me that Christ died for me.[5]

Nonetheless, these words did not thoroughly persuade Charles. He was so convinced that she had not previously been saved that when she later died, he had put on her tombstone that she had "lived a legal night of seventy years."

Regardless of what Charles thought about his mother, however, the facts of her spiritual life do not support his assumptions.

Two more examples will have to suffice. Twenty-five years before her experience at that poignant Communion service, Susanna Wesley wrote the following devotional concerning an inward faith:

To know God only as a philosopher; to have the most sublime and curious speculations concerning His essence, His attributes, His Providence; to be able to demonstrate His being from all or any of the works of nature;

---

[5]Ibid., 164.

and to discourse with the greatest elegancy and propriety of words His existence or operations will avail us nothing, unless at the same time we know Him experimentally; unless the heart perceive and know Him to be its supreme good, its only happiness; unless the soul feel and acknowledge that she can find no repose, no peace, no joy, but in loving and being beloved by Him; and does accordingly rest in Him as the center of her being, the fountain of her pleasure, the origin of all virtue and goodness, her light, her life, her strength, her all; everything she wants or wishes in this world, and forever!

In a word, HER LORD, HER GOD! Thus, let me ever know Thee, O God! I do not despise or neglect the light of reason or that knowledge of Thee which by her conduct may be collected from this goodly system of created beings, but this speculative knowledge is not the knowledge I want and wish for.[6]

If to esteem and have the highest reverence for Thee; if constantly and sincerely to acknowledge Thee the supreme, the only desirable good, be to love Thee, I DO LOVE THEE! If to rejoice in Thy essential majesty and glory; if to feel a vital joy overspread and cheer the heart at each perception of Thy blessedness, at every thought that Thou art God and that all things are in Thy power; that there is none superior or equal to Thee, be to love Thee, I DO LOVE THEE! If comparatively to despise and undervalue all the world contains, which is esteemed great, fair, or good; if earnestly and constantly to desire Thee, Thy favor, Thy acceptance, Thyself, rather than any or all things Thou hast created, be to love Thee, I DO LOVE THEE![7]

These two writings serve as ample evidence to support the fact that Susanna possessed a strong biblical

[6]Kirk, 266–267.
[7]Ibid., 267.

faith long before January 1740.

There is another reason why the brothers questioned their mother's claim of early conversion. It has to do with a conversation John had with her a year before the Communion service.

The following is a short excerpt about that conversation taken from John's journal. The entry was made on September 3, 1739:

> I talked largely with my mother, who told me that, till a short time ago, she had scarce heard such a thing mentioned as having forgiveness of sins now, or God's Spirit bearing witness with our spirit: much less did she believe that this was the common privilege of all believers. "Therefore," said she, "I never dared to ask it for myself."

Susanna went on to tell John that after her experience with the sacramental cup she felt this assurance. She knew that her father had the joy of this assurance for more than forty years. But since he never preached it to the people, she thought it was a blessing reserved for only a chosen few.

Be that as it may, because Susanna did not fully understand the concept of justification by faith or the idea of the assurance of salvation, does not mean she was not a true believer. As Adam Clarke points out:

> She lived in a time when the spiritual privileges of the people of God were not so clearly defined, nor so well understood as they are at present; yet she was not without large communications of the divine Spirit. . . . She had the faith of God's elect; she acknowledged the truth that is according to godliness. Her spirit and life were conformed to the truth; and she was not, as she could not be, without the favor and approbation of God.[8]

---

[8]Clarke, 415.

Susanna Wesley's faith, then, was not newly discovered at the Communion service in January 1740, but was more clearly defined. She now understood the assurance of her salvation and experienced the joy of that security.

This revitalized faith enabled her to endure another tragedy. On March 9, 1741, at thirty years of age, her youngest daughter, Kezia, died. Susanna was deeply saddened, but at the same time she rejoiced that Kezia passed away without too much "pain or trouble."

In July 1742 Susanna herself lay on her deathbed. In the following account taken from his journal, John described her last few days on earth:

I left Bristol on the evening of Sunday, July 18, 1742, and on Tuesday came to London. I found my mother on the borders of eternity, but she had no doubts or fear or any desire but that as soon as God should call "to depart and be with Christ."

Friday, July 23. About three in the afternoon I went to see my mother, and found her change was near. I sat down on the bedside; she was in her last conflict, unable to speak, but I believe quite conscious. Her look was calm and serene, and her eyes fixed upward, while we commended her soul to God.

From three to four the silver cord was loosing, and the wheel breaking at the cistern; and then, without any struggle, or sigh, or groan, the soul was set at liberty. We stood round the bed and fulfilled her last request, which had been uttered a little before she lost her speech, "Children, as soon as I am released, sing a psalm of praise to God."

Sunday, August 1. Almost an innumerable company of people being gathered together, about five in the afternoon I committed to the earth the body of my mother, to sleep with her fathers. The portion of Scripture from which I afterward spoke was, "I saw a great white throne, and him that sat on it, from whose face the earth and the heaven fled away, and there was found no place for them.

And I saw the dead small and great stand before God, and the books were opened. And the dead were judged out of those things which were written in the books according to their works." It was one of the most solemn assemblies I ever saw, or expect to see, this side of eternity.

We set up a plain stone at the head of her grave, inscribed with the following words:

> Here lies the body of Mrs. Susanna Wesley,
> the youngest and last surviving daughter
> of Dr. Samuel Annesley.
> In sure and steadfast hope to rise
> And claim her mansion in the skies,
> A Christian here her flesh laid down,
> The cross exchanging for a crown.
> True daughter of affliction, she,
> Inured to pain and misery,
> Mourn'd a long night of griefs and fears,
> A legal night of seventy years:
> The Father then reveal'd his Son,
> Him in the broken bread made known;
> She knew and felt her sins forgiven,
> And found the earnest of heaven.
> Meet for the fellowship above,
> She heard the call, "Arise my love."
> "I come," her dying looks replied,
> And lamblike, as her Lord, she died.[9]

Several years later, Susanna's tombstone was changed to reflect her role as the faithful wife of Samuel Wesley and the loving mother of John and Charles Wesley, the founders of Methodism:

---

[9]John Wesley, *Journal*, vol. 3, 29–31.

Here lies the body of
MRS. SUSANNA WESLEY,
Widow of the Rev. Samuel Wesley, M.A.,
(late Rector of Epworth, in Lincolnshire,)
who died July 23, 1742,
aged 73 years.
She was the youngest daughter of the
Rev. Samuel Annesley, D.D.,
ejected by the Act of Uniformity
from the Rectory of St. Giles's,
Cripplegate, August 24, 1662.
She was the mother of nineteen children,
of whom the most eminent were the
REV. JOHN WESLEY AND CHARLES WESLEY;
the former of whom was under God the
founder of the Societies of the People
called Methodists.[10]

Anyone who has ever studied the life of Susanna Wesley has come away with a deep sense of awe and wonder. Adam Clarke summed it up best when he said,

I have traced her life with much pleasure, and received from it much instruction; and when I have seen her repeatedly grappling with gigantic adversities, I have adored the grace of God that was in her, and have not been able to repress my tears. I have been acquainted with many pious females; I have read the lives of several others, and composed memoirs of a few; but such a woman, take her for all in all, I have not heard of, I have not read of, nor with her equal have I been acquainted. Such a one Solomon has described in the last chapter of his Proverbs; and to her I can apply the summed-up character of his accomplished housewife: Many daughters have done virtuously; but SUSANNA

---

[10]Clarke, 420.

WESLEY has excelled them all.[11]

As Susanna Wesley's life has unfolded before you, our hope is that you have been not only moved by her undaunted faith and determination but also inspired to follow her godly example.

---

[11]Adam Clarke, *Memoirs of the Wesley Family* (New York: Lane & Tippett, 1848), 420.

Appendix 1
Susanna Wesley's Exposition on the Apostle's Creed

I BELIEVE IN GOD

I do truly and heartily assent to the being of a God, one supreme, independent Power, who is a Spirit infinitely wise, holy, good, just, true, unchangeable.

I do believe that this God is a necessary, self-existent Being; necessary, in that he could not but be because he derives his existence from no other than himself; but he always is

THE FATHER

And having all life, all being in himself, all creatures must derive their existence from him; from what source he is properly styled the Father of all things, more especially of all spiritual natures, angels, and souls of men: and since he is the great Parent of the universe, it naturally follows that he is

---

ALMIGHTY

And this glorious attribute of his omnipotence is evident in that he has the right to make anything he wills after that manner which best pleases him, according to the absolute freedom of his own will; and the right to possess all things so made by him as he pleases: nor can his almighty, infinite power admit any weakness, dependence, or limitation, but it extends to all things.

It is boundless, incomprehensible, and eternal. And though we cannot comprehend or have any adequate conception of what so far surpasses the human understanding, yet it is plainly evident that he is omnipotent from his being the

MAKER OF HEAVEN AND EARTH

Of all things visible: nor could anything less than almighty power produce the smallest, most inconsiderable thing out of nothing. Not the least blade of grass or most despicable insect, but bears the divine signature and carries in its existence a clear demonstration of the Deity.

For could we admit of such a wild supposition as that anything could make itself, it must necessarily follow that a thing had being before it had being, that it could act before it was, which is a obvious contradiction; from what cause, among other reasons, we conclude that this beautiful world, that celestial arch over our heads, and all those glorious heavenly bodies: sun, moon, stars, in short, the whole system of the universe, were in the beginning made or created out of nothing by the everblessed God, according to the counsel of his own will; or, as Paul better expresses it, "By him were all things created, that are in heaven, and that are in earth, visible and invisible, whether they be thrones, or dominions, or principalities, or powers: all things were created by him" (Col. 1:16).

IN JESUS

Jesus signifies a Savior; and by that name he was called by the angel Gabriel before his birth to show us that he came into the world to save us from our sins and the punishment they justly deserve, and to repair the damage human nature had sustained by the fall of Adam; that as in Adam all died, so in Christ all should be made alive: and so he became the second general Head of all humankind.

And as he was promised to our parents in paradise, so was his coming signified by the various types and sacrifices under the law and foretold by the prophets long before he appeared in the world.

And this Savior, this Jesus, was the promised Messiah, who was so long the hope and expectation of the Jews, the

CHRIST

Which, in the original, signifies anointed. Now among the Jews it was a custom to anoint three sorts of persons: prophets, priests, and kings; which anointing did not only show their designation to those offices but was also usually attended with a special influence or inspiration of the Holy Spirit to prepare and qualify them for such offices.

Our blessed Lord, who was by his almighty Father sanctified and sent into the world, was also anointed, not with material oil, but by the descent of the Holy Spirit upon him, to signify to us that he was our Prophet, Priest, and King; and that he should first, as our Prophet, fully and clearly reveal the will of God for our salvation, which accordingly he did.

And though the Jews had long before received the law by Moses, yet a great part of that law was purely typical and ceremonial, and all of it was necessarily vacated by the coming of our Savior; and that part which was moral, and consequently of perpetual obligation, they had so corrupted by their misrepresentations and various traditions that it was not as pure and undefiled as God delivered it on Mount Sinai, which occasioned the words of our Lord,

"Think not that I have come to destroy the law and the prophets; I am not come to destroy, but to fulfill": to accomplish the predictions of the prophets concerning himself and to rescue the moral law from the false glosses they had placed on it.

Though the rest of the world were not altogether without some precept of morality, yet they lay scattered up and down in the writings of a few wiser and better than the rest: but morality was never collected into a complete system till the coming of our Savior; nor was life and immortality brought fully to light till the preaching of the Gospel.

He is our Priest, in that he offered up himself a sacrifice to divine justice in our stead; and by the perfect satisfaction he made, he did atone the displeasure of God and purchase eternal life for us, which was forfeited by the first man's disobedience.

And as he is our Prophet and Priest, so likewise he is our King, and has an unquestionable right to govern those he has redeemed by his blood, and as such he will conquer for us all our spiritual enemies, sin, and death, and all the powers of the kingdom of darkness; and when he has perfectly subdued them, he will actually confer upon us eternal happiness.

This satisfaction and purchase that Christ has made for us is a clear proof of his divinity, since no mere man is capable of meriting anything good from God; and therefore we are obliged to consider him in a state of equality with the Father, being

HIS ONLY SON

Though we are children of the almighty Father, yet he has only one Son, by an eternal and incomprehensible generation, which only Son is Jesus the Savior, being equal with the Father in the Godhead but inferior to the Father in his manhood: God of God, Light of Light, Very God of Very God; begotten, not made. And this only Son of God we acknowledge to be

OUR LORD

In that he is coequal and coessential with the Father, and by him were all things made. Therefore, since we are his creatures, we must with the apostle Thomas confess him to be our Lord and our God. But besides this right to our allegiance, which he has by creation, he has redeemed us from death and hell and he has purchased us with his own blood: so that upon a double account we justly call him Lord, namely, that of creation and of purchase.

And as the infinite condescension of the eternal Son of God in assuming our nature was mysterious and incomprehensible, surpassing the wisest of men or angels to conceive how such a thing might be; so it was required and agreeable to the majesty of God that the conception of his sacred person should be after a manner altogether differing from ordinary generations; accordingly it was he

WHO WAS CONCEIVED BY THE HOLY SPIRIT

Whose miraculous conception was foretold by the angel, when his blessed mother questioned how she who was a virgin could conceive: "The Holy Spirit shall come upon you, and the power of the Most High shall over-shadow you; therefore also that holy child which shall be born of you shall be called the Son of God." And as all the sacrifices that represented our Savior under the law were to be without spot or blemish, so likewise Christ, the great Christian sacrifice, was infinitely pure and holy, not only in his divine, but also in his human nature; he was perfectly immaculate, having none but God for his Father, being

BORN OF THE VIRGIN MARY

Whose spotless purity no age of the catholic church has presumed to question. That the promised Messiah should be born of a virgin is plain from Jeremiah 31:22, "The Lord hath created a new thing in the earth, A woman shall compass a man." And from Isaiah 7:14, "Behold, a virgin shall conceive, and bear a son, and shall call his name Immanuel."

And this seed of the woman must necessarily have assumed our nature, or he could never have been our Jesus, the Savior of the world; for the divine nature of the Son of God is infinitely happy, utterly incapable of any grief, pain, or sense of misery.

Nor could its union with humanity in any way defile or pollute it, or deviate the least from its infinite perfection: so it was only as man that he

SUFFERED

Those infirmities and calamities incident to human nature. What transactions passed between the almighty Father and his eternal Son concerning the redemption of the world, we know not; but we are sure that by an express agreement between them he was from eternity decreed to suffer for humankind.

And in several places of the Old Testament it is written of the Son of man that he must suffer many things. And the Spirit of Christ that was in the prophets testified beforehand the sufferings of Christ; particularly in Isaiah 53, we have a sad but clear description of the sufferings of the Messiah.

Indeed, his whole life was one continual scene of misery. No sooner was he born, than he was persecuted by Herod and forced to flee into Egypt, in the arms of a weak virgin, under the protection of a foster father. And when he returned into his own country, he for thirty years lived in a low condition, probably employed in the mean trade of a carpenter, which made him in the eyes of the world despicable, of no reputation.

And when, after so long an obscurity, he appeared unto men, he entered upon his ministry with the severity of forty days abstinence.

Behold, the eternal Lord of nature was transported into a wild and desolate wilderness, exposed to the severity of the air, and tempted by the apostate spirits!

The almighty Being, who justly claims a right to the whole creation, was himself hungry and thirsty; often wearied with painful traveling from place to place. And though he went about doing good, and never sent anyone away from him who wanted relief, without healing their diseases and casting out those evil spirits that afflicted them, yet was he despised and rejected of men!

The Possessor of heaven and earth, the sovereign Giver of all things, from whose bounty all creatures receive what they enjoy of the necessary accommodations of life, was reduced to such a mean estate, that the foxes had holes and the birds of the air had nests, yet the Son of man had no place to lay his head! All his life he was a man of sorrows and acquainted with grief, yet his greatest sufferings were

UNDER PONTIUS PILATE

Who was at that time the Roman governor of Judea, under Tiberius, the emperor of Rome. His office was that of a procurator, whose business it was not only to take an account of the tribute due to the emperor, and to order and dispose of the same to his advantage, but by means of the seditious and rebellious temper of the Jews they were further trusted with some supreme powers among them: a power of life and death, which was a signal instance of divine providence and a clear proof of the predictions of the prophets, which had long before foretold that the Messiah should suffer after a manner that was not prescribed by the law of Moses. And this circumstance of time is mentioned to confirm the truth of our Savior's history.

And now behold a mysterious scene of wonders indeed! The immaculate Lamb of God, who came to save the world from misery, under the greatest, most amazing apprehensions of his approaching passion! "He began to be sorrowful," says Matthew; "To be sore amazed, and very heavy," says Mark.

His soul was pressed with fear, horror, and dejection of mind; tormented with anxiety, and uneasiness of spirit, which he expressed to his disciples in these sad words: "My soul is exceeding sorrowful, even unto death!" See him retire to a solitary garden at a still, gloomy hour of the night!

Behold him prostrate on the ground, conflicting with the wrath of his almighty Father! He perfectly knew what God is, the severe purity of the Deity, and was absolutely conformed to his will.

He knew the evil of sin, in its nature and consequences; the perfect justice, wisdom, and goodness of the divine laws. He understood the inexpressible misery man had brought upon himself by the violation of them, and how intolerable it would be for man to sustain the vengeance of an angry God; and perhaps he was moved with extreme concern and pity, when he foresaw that, notwithstanding all he had already done and was then about to suffer for his salvation, there would be so many that would obstinately perish!

He had a full prospect of all he had yet to undergo; that the conflict was not yet over, but that the dregs of that bitter cup still remained; that he must be forsaken of his Father in the midst of his torments, which made him three times so earnestly repeat his petition that if it were possible the cup might pass from him. But the full complement of his sufferings, we may suppose, was that he actually sustained the whole weight of that grief and sorrow due the justice of God for the sins of the whole world.

And this, we may believe, caused that inconceivable agony, when his sweat was as great drops of blood falling to the ground. And though his torments were so inexpressibly great, yet the Son of man suffered many things. He was betrayed by one disciple, denied by another, and forsaken by all.

And as he suffered in his soul, by the most intense grief and anguish, so he had to suffer in his body the greatest bitterness of corporeal pains that the malice and rage of his enemies could inflict upon it. And now the sovereign Lord and Judge of all men is haled before the tribunal of his sinful creatures; the pure, unspotted Son of God, who could do no wrong, neither could guile be found in his mouth, was accused by his presumptuous slaves of no less a crime than blasphemy.

And though the witnesses could by no means agree together, and he was so often declared innocent by Pilate, an infidel judge, yet still the rude and barbarous rabble, being instigated by the envy and malice of the chief priests and elders, persist in demanding that he should be condemned.

And when, in compliance with their usual custom of having a criminal released at their feast, Pilate, in order to save him, proposed his release instead of Barabbas, who was a seditious murderer, yet they persisted in their fury and preferred the murderer before the Prince of life and glory; nor would they be satisfied till he

WAS CRUCIFIED

To which humiliating death the Romans commonly condemned their greatest criminals. It was considered so vile and so shameful among them, that it was deemed a very high crime to put any free man to death after such a dishonorable manner; and as the shame was great, so it was usually accompanied with many previous pains.

They were first cruelly scourged, and then compelled to bear their cross on their bleeding wounds to the place of crucifixion; all which the meek and patient Jesus underwent cheerfully for his love toward mankind.

The scourgers ploughed on his back and made long their furrows. But there were other painful circumstances that attended and increased the sufferings of our Savior. They had not only accused him of blasphemy but of treason and sedition: "We found this fellow perverting the nation, and forbidding to give tribute to Caesar, saying, that he himself was Christ, a king;" which, as it moved Pilate to condemn him, so it moved the rude soldiers to insult him by their mock banners of royalty.

They arrayed him in a purple robe and put a reed in his hand, and they bowed the knee before him, saying, "Hail, King of the Jews!" And the crown of thorns, which they wove together and put on his head, not only expressed the scorn of his tormentors but did, by the piercing of his sacred temples, cause exquisite pain.

That blessed face, which angels rejoice to behold, they buffeted and spat upon; nor was any circumstance of cruelty, which their witty malice could suggest to torment him, omitted by those inhuman rebels, till, wearied with their own barbarity, and impatient of his living any longer, they put his own clothes on him again and led him away to crucifixion.

And now let us, by faith, attend our Lord to his last scene of misery. Let us ascend with him to the top of Mount Calvary, and see with what cruel pleasure they nail his hands and feet to the infamous wood, which after having done so, they raise him from the earth, and the whole weight of his body is sustained by those four wounds.

But though the corporeal pains occasioned by the thorns, the scourging, the piercing of those nerve-filled and sensitive parts of his most sacred body, were wrought up to an inexpressible degree of torture, yet were they infinitely surpassed by the anguish of his soul when there was (after what manner we cannot conceive) a sensible withdrawing of the comfortable presence of the Deity, which caused that loud and impassioned exclamation, "My God, my God, why hast thou forsaken me?"

And now it is finished: the measure of his suffering is completed; and he, who could not die but by his own voluntary act of resigning life, gave up his pure and spotless soul into the hands of his almighty Father. And though senseless men could look insensitively on the mysterious passion of their blessed Redeemer, yet nature could not so behold her dying Lord, but by strong commotions expressed her sympathy.

The sun, as if ashamed and astonished at the barbarous inhumanity and ingratitude of man, withdrew his influence; nor would he display the brightness of his beams when the great Son of God lay under the eclipse of death.

The foundations of the solid earth were shaken, the rocks split, and the graves were opened; and the veil of the temple was torn in two from top to bottom, signifying that all, both Jews and Gentiles, have free admission into the Holy of Holies, into the haven of his presence, through the blood of Jesus, which extorted a confession of his divinity even from his enemies; for when the centurion and they that were with him, watching Jesus, saw the earthquake and those things that were done, they feared greatly, saying, "Truly, this was the Son of God."

Now, though crucifixion does not necessarily mean certain death, but that if a person be taken from the cross he may live; yet, since it is evident that the Messiah was to die, and that for that cause he was born and come into the world, that he might, by the grace of God, suffer death for every man, so we are bound to believe that he was truly

DEAD

And as his death was foretold, so likewise his burial was typified by the prophet Jonah; for as he was three days and three nights in the belly of the whale, so was the Son of man three days and three nights in the heart of the earth.

And though by Roman law those who were crucified were not allowed the favor of a grave, but were to remain on the cross, exposed to the fowls of the air and the beasts of the field, yet it was in the power of the magistrate to permit a burial; and the providence of God had so ordered it, that those very persons who had caused him to be crucified should petition for his being taken down from the cross; for the law of Moses required, that "if a man have committed a sin worthy of death, and you hang him on a tree, his body shall not remain all night upon the tree, but you shall bury him that night."

And therefore they begged of Pilate that the body should be taken down from the cross; and this was the first step toward our Savior's burial. "And when evening came, because it was the preparation, that is, the day before the Sabbath, Josèph of Arimathea, an honorable counselor, which also waited for the kingdom of God, came and went in boldly to Pilate and asked for the body of Jesus. And he gave the body to Joseph; and he brought fine linen, wrapped him in the linen, and laid him in a grave that was cut out of rock, wherein never man before was laid, and rolled a stone to the door of the grave, and departed."

HE DESCENDED INTO HELL

That our blessed Lord did actually descend into hell, seems very plain from Peter's exposition of that text in the Psalms: "You shall not leave my soul in hell, neither shall you let your Holy One see corruption"; when, having mentioned this passage, he thus explains it: "He, (that is, David) seeing this before, (namely, the incarnation of the Son of God) spoke of his resurrection; that his soul was not left in hell, neither did his flesh see corruption"; which is clear proof that his soul did actually descend into hell after it was separated from his body. But though he underwent the condition of a sinner in this world, and suffered and died as a sinner, yet being perfectly holy, and having, by virtue of the union of the Deity to his human nature, fully satisfied the strictest demands of divine justice, we are not to suppose that he either did or could suffer the torments of the damned; therefore, we may reasonably conclude that his descent into hell was not to suffer, but to triumph over principalities and powers; over the rulers of the kingdom of darkness, in their own sad regions of horror and despair;

and for this reason, and in this sense, are we to understand his descent into hell.

And as his soul was not left in hell, neither did his flesh see corruption; but having by his own almighty power loosed the pain of death, because it was impossible that he should be held by it,

THE THIRD DAY HE ROSE AGAIN FROM THE DEAD

Friday, on which he suffered, and the first day of the week, on which he rose, are included in the number of the three days. And this first day of the week the apostles and primitive Christians have ever since observed as the Sabbath.

That as the Jews, who will not believe in any greater deliverance than that of Egypt, still keep the seventh day, and the Turks Friday, in memory of Mohammed's flight from Mecca, whom they esteem a greater prophet than Christ or Moses; so all Christians are distinguished from the rest of the world by their observance of the first day, in commemoration of our Savior's rising from the dead and his finishing the great work of man's redemption on that day.

Thus, we believe, that as Christ died for our sins, was buried, and rose again the third day, according to the Scriptures; so,

HE ASCENDED INTO HEAVEN

He had for forty days after his resurrection remained upon earth, during which time he appeared frequently to his disciples, ate and drank with them, showed them the marks of his crucifixion, to convince them that it was the same body that suffered for our offenses that was raised for our justification; and that by his so doing we might have a sure and certain hope of our own resurrection from the dead. And when he had spoken to his disciples and blessed them, he parted from them and ascended into the highest heaven, where he still remains,

AND SITS ON THE RIGHT HAND OF GOD, THE FATHER ALMIGHTY

God is Spirit, nor has he any body, so he cannot properly be said to have any parts, such as eyes, ears, hands, as we see bodies have; therefore, we may suppose that the right hand of God signifies his exceeding great and infinite power and glory.

And Christ is said to sit down on the right hand of God in regard to that absolute power and dominion that he has obtained in heaven; accordingly, as he told the Jews, "From now on you shall see the Son of man sitting on the right hand of power."

After all the labor, sorrow, shame, contempt, and torment he suffered in this world, he rests above in a permanent state of endless glory and unspeakable bliss; and,

THEREFORE, HE SHALL COME TO JUDGE THE QUICK AND THE DEAD

All that shall be found alive at his coming, as well as those that have died since Adam, shall appear before the judgment seat of Christ, to be by him judged according to what they have done on earth; to be by him determined and sentenced and finally disposed to their eternal condition.

Those that have done well he shall receive into everlasting life, to remain forever with him in eternal blessedness; and those that have done evil he shall condemn to the kingdom of darkness, there to remain in unimaginable misery forever with the devil and his angels.

And as we must thus profess to believe in God the Father, and in Jesus Christ his only Son, so we must every-one truly and heartily say,

I BELIEVE IN THE HOLY SPIRIT

That he is a person, of a real and true subsistence, neither created nor begotten, but proceeding from the Father and the Son; true and eternal God, who is essentially holy himself, and the author of all holiness in us, by sanctifying our natures, illuminating our minds, rectifying our wills and affections; who cooperates with the Word and the Sacraments, and whatever else is a means of conveying grace unto the soul.

It was he that spoke by the prophets and apostles, and it is he who leads us into all truth. He helps our infirmities, assures us of our adoption, and will be with

THE HOLY CATHOLIC CHURCH

To the end of the world. The catholic church is composed of all congregations of men and women who hold the faith of Jesus Christ and are obedient to his laws, wherein the pure Word of God is preached and the Sacraments duly delivered by such ministers as are regularly consecrated and set apart for such ordinances, according to Christ's institution.

And as this church is called holy in respect of its author, Jesus: the end, the glory of God and the salvation of men, the institution of the ministry, the administration of the Sacraments, the preaching of the pure Word of God; and of the members of this church, who are renewed and sanctified by the Holy Spirit, and united to Christ, the supreme Head and Governor of the church.

It is called catholic, because it is not, like that of the

Jews, confined to one place and people, but is disseminated through all nations, extends throughout all ages, even to the end of the world. And as there is but one Head; so the members, though many, are one body, united together by the same spirit, principally by the three great Christian virtues: faith, hope, and charity.

For as we hold the same principles of faith, we do all assent to the same hopes and expectations of eternal life that are promised to all. And as our Lord gave the same mark of distinction to all his disciples, "By this shall all men know that you are my disciples, if you love one another," so this universal love, which is diffused throughout the whole body of Christ, is the union of charity; and the same ministry and the same orders in the church make the unity of discipline.

But since Christ has appointed only one way to heaven; so we are not to expect salvation out of the church, which is called catholic, in opposition to heretics and schismatics. And if an angel from heaven should preach any other doctrine than that which Christ and his apostles have taught, or appoint any other Sacraments than those which Christ has already instituted, let him be accursed.

And as the mystical union between Christ and the church, and the spiritual conjunction of the members with the Head, is the fountain of that union and communion which the saints have with each other, as being all under the influence of the same Head; so death, which only separates bodies for a time, cannot dissolve the union of minds; and therefore it is not only in relation to the saints on earth but including also those in heaven, we profess to hold

THE COMMUNION OF THE SAINTS

Accordingly, we believe that all saints, those on earth as well as those in heaven, have communion with God the

Father, Son, and Holy Spirit; with the blessed angels, who not only join in devotion with the church triumphant above but are likewise gone forth to minister to those who are the heirs of salvation while they remain in this world.

And perhaps we do not consider as we ought how much good we receive by the ministration of the holy angels; nor are we sufficiently grateful to those guardian spirits that so often save us from accidents, watch over us when we sleep, defending us from the assault of evil men and evil angels.

And if they are so mindful of our preservation in this world, we may suppose them much more concerned for our eternal happiness: "There is joy among the angels in heaven over one sinner that repents."

They are present in our public assemblies, where we in a more special manner hold communion with them; and it is there that we join with all the company of the heavenly host in praising and admiring the Supreme Being, whom we jointly adore. What knowledge the saints in heaven have of things or persons in this world, we cannot determine, nor after what manner we hold communion with them, it is not at present easy to conceive.

That we are all members of the same mystical body, Christ, we are very sure; and do all partake of the same vital influence from the same Head, and so we are united together; and though we are not actually possessed of the same happiness that they enjoy, yet we have the same Holy Spirit given unto us as an earnest of our eternal bliss with them hereafter.

And though their faith is consummated by vision, and their hope by present possession, yet the bond of Christian charity still remains; and as we have great joy and pleasure in their bliss, so, no doubt, they desire and pray for us.

With the saints on earth we hold communion by the

Word and the Sacraments, by praying with and for each other; and in all acts of public or private worship we act upon the same principles and the same motives, having the same promises and hopes of

THE FORGIVENESS OF SINS

Through Jesus Christ, the Mediator of the new covenant, who gave his life a sacrifice by way of compensation and satisfaction to divine justice, by which God became reconciled to man, and canceled the obligation that every sinner lay under to suffer eternal punishment; and he has appointed in his church baptism for the first remission, and repentance for the constant forgiveness of all following trespasses.

And now have we confidence toward God, that not only our souls shall be freed from the guilt and punishment of sin by faith in Jesus but also our bodies may rest in hope of

THE RESURRECTION OF THE BODY

That the same almighty power that raised again our blessed Lord, after he had lain three days in the grave, shall again quicken our mortal bodies; shall reproduce the same individual body that slept in the dust, and vitally unite it to the same soul that inhabited it while on earth.

"The hour is coming, in the which all that are in the graves shall hear his voice, and shall come forth; they that have done good, unto the resurrection of life; and they that have done evil, unto the resurrection of damnation" (John 5:28–29).

"And the sea gave up the dead which were in it; and death and hell [that is, the grave] delivered up the dead which were in them" (Rev. 20:13). There shall be a general rendezvous of every particular atom that composed the several bodies of men and women that ever lived in the world; and each shall be restored to its proper owner, so as to make the same numerical body, the same flesh and blood, which were dissolved at death.

And though the bodies of the saints shall be glorified, heavenly bodies, yet they shall be of the same consistency and figure, but only altered and changed in some properties. And though at the first view it may seem hard to conceive how those bodies, which have suffered so many various changes, have either been buried in the earth, devoured by beasts, consumed by fire, or swallowed up in the sea; have been dissolved into the smallest atoms, and those atoms perhaps scattered throughout the world; have fertilized the earth, fed the fishes, and by that means become the food of animals and other men, and a part of their nourishment, till at last the same particles of matter belong to several bodies: how, I say, the same numerical atoms should at last rally and meet again, and be restored to the first owner, make up again the same first body, which so long since was consumed, may seem difficult, if not altogether impossible, to determine.

But since God has declared that he will raise the dead, we have no manner of reason to question whether he can do it, since omnipotence knows no difficulty; and that almighty power which first made us of nothing, out of no preexisting matter, can easily distinguish, and perceive, and unmix from other bodies our scattered atoms, and can recollect and unite them again, how far whatsoever they may be dispersed asunder.

He can observe the various changes they undergo in their passages through other bodies, and can so order it that they shall never become any part of their nourishment; or if they should be adopted into other men, he can cause them to yield them up again before they die, that they may be restored to their right owners; and having collected these particles, he can readily dispose them into the same order; rebuild the same beauteous fabric, consisting of the same flesh and bones, nerves, veins, blood, and all the several parts it had before its dissolution; and by reuniting it to the same soul, make the same living man.

But though the body shall be in substance the same after its resurrection as it was before its death, yet it shall greatly differ in its quality. "It was sown in corruption, it shall be raised in incorruption; it is sown in dishonor, it is raised in glory; it is sown in weakness, it is raised in power; it is sown a natural body, it is raised a spiritual body."

They shall not retain the same principles of corruption and mortality that they had before; they shall never die. The bodies of the damned shall eternally remain in the most inconceivable torment, while those of the blessed shall meet the Lord in the air when he comes to judgment, and afterward ascend with him into heaven, there to enjoy

THE LIFE EVERLASTING

By everlasting life is not only meant that we shall die no more; for in this sense the damned shall have everlasting life as well as the saints: they shall always have being, though in intolerable torment, which is infinitely worse than none at all.

But we are to understand by the life everlasting a full and perfect enjoyment of solid, inexpressible joy and bliss. "Eye hath not seen, nor ear heard, neither hath it entered into the heart of man to conceive, what God has prepared for those that love him."

The soul shall be perfectly sanctified, nor shall it be possible to sin anymore. All its faculties shall be purified and exalted: the understanding shall be filled with beatific vision of the most holy Trinity; shall be illuminated, enlarged, and eternally employed and satisfied in the contemplation of the sublimest truths.

Here we see as in a glass, having a dark and imperfect perception of God; but there we shall behold him as he is, shall know as we are known. Not that we shall fully comprehend the divine nature, as he does ours; that is impossible, for he is infinite and incomprehensible, and we, though in heaven, shall be finite still; but our apprehension of his being and perfection shall be clear, just, and true.

We shall see him as he is; shall nevermore be troubled with misapprehensions or false conceptions of him. Those dark and mysterious methods of Providence that here puzzle and confound the wisest heads to reconcile them with his justice and goodness, shall be there unriddled in a moment; and we shall clearly perceive that all the evils that befall good men in this life were the corrections of a merciful Father; that the furnace of affliction, which now seems so hot and terrible to nature, was nothing more than a lightly and gracefully lit flame, which was not designed to consume us, but only to purge away our dross, to purify and prepare the mind for its abode among those blessed ones that passed through the same trials before us into the celestial paradise.

And we shall forever adore and praise that infinite power and goodness that safely conducted the soul through the rough waves of this tempestuous ocean to the calm haven of peace and everlasting tranquillity.

Nor shall we have the same enticements there which we had here; but shall clearly discern that our afflictions here were our choicest mercies.

Our wills shall no longer be averse from God's, but shall be forever lost in that of our blessed Creator's. No conflicts with unruly passions, no pain or misery, shall ever find admittance into that heavenly kingdom.

"God shall wipe away all tears from our eyes; and there shall be no more death, neither sorrow, nor crying; neither shall there be any more pain; for the former things are passed away. Then we shall hunger no more, neither thirst anymore; neither shall the sun light upon us, nor any heat; for the Lamb, who is in the midst of the throne, shall feed us, and shall lead us unto living fountains of water."

Far be it from us to think that the grace of God can be purchased with anything less precious than the BLOOD OF JESUS; but if it could, who that has the lowest degree of faith would not part with all things in this world to obtain that love for our dear Redeemer after which we so long and sigh?

Here we cannot watch one hour with Jesus, without weariness, failure of spirits, dejection of mind, and worldly regards that dampen our devotion and pollute the purity of our sacrifice.

What Christian here does not often feel and bewail the weight of the corrupt nature, the many infirmities that molest us in our way to glory? And how difficult it is to practice as we ought that great duty of self-denial; to take up our cross, and follow the Captain of our salvation without ever repining or murmuring!

If shame or confusion could enter those blessed mansions, how would our souls be ashamed and confounded at the review of our imperfect services, when we see them crowned with such an unproportionable reward! How shall we blush to behold that exceeding and eternal weight of glory that is conferred upon us for that little, or rather nothing, which we have done or suffered for our Lord!

That God who gave us being, that preserved us, that fed and clothed us in our passage through the world; and, what is infinitely more, that gave his only Son to die for us, and has by his grace purified and conducted us safely to his glory!

Oh, blessed faith! Mysterious love! How shall we then adore and praise what we cannot here apprehend aright! How will love and joy work in the soul! But I cannot express it, I cannot conceive it.

I have purposely omitted many arguments for the being of God, the divine authority of Scripture, the truth of revealed religion or future judgment. The last article I have left very imperfect, because I intend to write on all these subjects for the use of my children when I have more leisure. I shall only add a few words to prepare your mind for the second part of my discourse, obedience to the laws of God, which I shall quickly send you.

As the defilement of our natures is the source and origin of all our actual iniquities and transgressions of the laws of God; so the first regular step we can take toward amendment is to be deeply conscious of, grieved and humbled for, our original sin.

And though (I believe) the damning guilt of that sin is washed away by baptism, by those who die before they are capable of known and actual transgressions; yet experience shows us that the power of it does still survive in such as attain to riper years; and this is what the apostle complains of in Romans 7.

This is the carnal nature; that law in our members that wars against the law of the mind, and brings into captivity to the law of sin.

And when the work of conversion or regeneration is begun by the Holy Spirit, yet still the corrupt nature maintains a conflict with divine grace, nor shall this enemy be entirely conquered, till death shall be swallowed up in victory; till this mortal shall have put on immortality.

I cannot tell whether you have ever seriously considered the lost and miserable condition you are in by nature. If you have not, it is high time to begin to do it; and I shall earnestly beseech the Almighty to enlighten your mind, to renew and sanctify you by his Holy Spirit, that you may be his child by adoption here, and an heir of his blessed kingdom hereafter!

Susanna Wesley,
Epworth,
January 13, 1709–1710

Appendix 2
Select Meditations and Prayers
of Susanna Wesley

MORNING

Whenever company or business inclines you to quit your solitude, and either to omit or cursorily perform accustomed exercises of devotion; and you, instead of resisting, comply with such inclinations, you may observe that you are guilty of some sin or error that, upon reflection, gives you more pain than the profit or pleasure gave you satisfaction. Therefore, make it your duty to conquer your inclination to any distraction at such times; nor let any trivial business divert you; for no business, unless it cannot be laid aside or suspended without sin, can be of equal, much less of greater, importance than caring for the soul.

NOON

What can human reason do, or how far can the light of reason direct us to find the knowledge of the Most High? From the primordial of the universe we collect that there is one supreme, eternal, consequently self-existent,

Being, who gave being to all things, since to act presupposes existence; for nothing can act before it is being.

That this being must possess, by way of eminence, all the perfection we discern in creatures, reason tells us; for nothing can impart to another that which it has not to impart.

EVENING

That person who will readily believe an ill report of you never was, or at least is not now, your friend. Seneca, a heathen, could say, "In some cases I will not believe a man against himself. I will give him, however, time to recollect himself: nay, sometimes, I will allow him counsel too."

But Christians are rarely so candid. He is a friend indeed who is proof against slander; but he is a rare Christian that will not believe a man against himself.

"This is eternal life to know you, the only true God and Jesus Christ, whom you have sent." But what is it to know God? Or what is that knowledge of God on which eternal life depends?

MORNING

To know God as a man, as a reasonable creature, is not that knowledge that leads to eternal life. It is a knowledge of another kind, one attained by scientific method, by a long train of arguments, for which the bulk of mankind lacks either capacity or leisure. The knowledge that leads to eternal life is by frequent and fervent application to God in prayer.

The one is by effect of reason assisted by human learning, peculiar to a few of more noble and refined sense; God perceived, known to the understanding as the Creator, Preserver, and Governor of the universe.

The other is reason acting by the influence and direction of the Holy Spirit; God known to the heart, the will, and the affections, not merely as the Author of our being, but as he is exhibited to us under the character of the Healer and Repairer of the lapse and misery of human nature; a Savior, him whom our soul loves.

NOON

To know God only as a philosopher knows him; to have the most sublime and curious speculations concerning his essence, his attributes, his Providence; to be able to demonstrate his being from all or any of the works of nature, and to discourse with the greatest elegancy and propriety of words his existence or operations, will avail us nothing, unless at the same time we know him experimentally; unless the heart perceives and knows him to be its supreme good, its only happiness; unless the soul feels and acknowledges that she can find no repose, no peace, no joy but in loving and being beloved by him; and does accordingly rest in him as the center of her being, the fountain of her pleasure, the origin of all virtue and goodness, her light, her life, her strength, her all; everything she wants or wishes in this world, and forever: In a word, Her Lord, Her God.

Thus, let me ever know you, O God! I do not despise nor neglect the light of reason, nor that knowledge of you which by her conduct may be collected from this goodly system of created being; but this speculative knowledge is not the knowledge I wish for or want.

EVENING

And as creation demonstrates omnipotence, so that infers wisdom, justice, truth, purity, and goodness. For all these perfections are intellectual powers, and were

God deficient in one, he could not be omnipotent.

That he is a Spirit unbodied, undetermined, immense, filling heaven and earth, all the imaginary spaces beyond them; most simple, uncompounded, and absolutely separated and free from whatever pollution a spirit is capable of being defiled with; immutable, incapable of change or alteration for the better or worse; perfectly free, knowing no superior, no equal that may impel, allure, or persuade him, but acting always spontaneously according to the counsel of his own will, we may discover by the light of nature.

MORNING

It is very likely that your good humor last night was the effect of fancy and passion rather than that of a clear, sound judgment. If otherwise, why did you feel uneasiness at another person being out of humor? Was it not pride that made you resent contradiction?

Or from what other principle could that reluctance flow, which you felt in obeying a trivial command, which perhaps might proceed from fretfulness? Yet the matter being indifferent, obedience was unquestionably your duty.

A wise person ought seldom, or indeed ever, when authority is not disputed or condemned, perform acts of power because they are shocking to human nature; which, if not fortified and strengthened by religion, is apt in such cases to throw off all subjection and rebel against even lawful government.

But though you should meet with high instances, which the pride of humankind will throw in your way; yet take care not to swerve from your duty. Look upon every such act as a call of divine Providence to exercise the virtues of meekness and humility.

When you can bear severe reflections, unjust censures, contemptuous words, and unreasonable actions without perturbation, without rendering evil for evil, but can with an equal temper clearly discern and cheerfully do your duty, you may hope that God has given you some degree of humility and resignation.

EVENING

The philosophy of the whole world has not sufficient force to conquer the tendency toward corrupt nature. Appetites and passions will bear sway, in spite of all our fine speculations, until our minds are enlightened by some higher principle. By virtue of that light the mind discerns the moral depravity of those things in which before it placed its supreme happiness, and the beauty of that virtue and holiness to which it was before accustomed to despise.

MORNING

Commit your soul morning and evening to Jesus Christ, as he is the Savior of the world. Then observe what he says unto you, resolutely obey his precepts, and endeavor to follow his example in those things wherein he has exhibited to you a pattern for your imitation.

There is no circumstance or time of life but that you may find something either spoken by our Lord himself or by his Spirit through the prophets or apostles that will direct your conduct, if you are but faithful to God and to your own soul.

EVENING

There are great obstacles in the way of Christian perfection. What says our Lord through his apostle John? "Love not the world; if any man love the world, the love of the Father is not in him." That one will as certainly be damned whose affections are fixed on sensual pleasures, riches, or honors, even though that one never enjoys any, or a very inconsiderable proportion of them, as having them all in one's power, indulges in the satisfaction of one's most criminal desires.

For 'tis the heart God requires, and if we suffer our heart to center on anything but God, the object of our passion, innocent or otherwise, will actually make that thing our god, and in so doing forfeit our title and pretensions to eternal happiness.

MORNING

Another great impediment is deep adversity, which often affects the mind too much and disposes it to anxious, doubtful, and unbelieving thoughts.

Though there be no direct murmurings, no complaining at the prosperity of others, no harsh reflections on Providence, but a constant acknowledgment of the justice and goodness of God; that he punishes less than our iniquities deserve, and does always in the midst of judgment remember mercy; yet if you think severely or unjustly of others; if you are too much dejected or disposed to fretfulness, covetousness, or negligence in affairs; if you work too much or too little, are presumptuous or desponding; wholly negligent to implore the divine blessing and assistance on honest prospects and endeavors; or are too anxiously desirous and earnest in prayer for external blessings; if the thought of your circumstances invade your privacy or disturb your rest; if any little access of trouble has the power to ruffle your temper and indispose or distract your mind in your addresses to heaven, in reading, meditation, or any other spiritual exercise, you are certainly in the power of the world, guilty of immoderate, anxious care.

Then observe what your Lord says by his apostle: "Be anxious for nothing." And what he says himself, "Therefore, I say unto you, take no thought. . . ." and remember that he ranks cares of this life with overindulgence and drunkenness, which are mortal, damning sins.

MORNING

The great difficulty we find in restraining our appetites and passions from excess often arises from the liberties we take in indulging them in all those instances wherein there does not at first sight appear some moral evil. Occasions of sin frequently take their rise from lawful enjoyments; and if we always venture to the utmost bounds of what we may, we will not fail to step beyond the boundary sometimes; and then we may use our liberty for a cloak of licentiousness.

He that habitually knows and abhors the sin of indulgence, will not stay too long in the company of such as are indulgent. . . .

It holds the same in all other irregular appetites or passions; and there may be the same temptations in other instances from whence occasions of sin may arise; therefore, be sure to keep a strict guard, and observe well lest you use lawful pleasures unlawfully. "Fly from occasions of evil."

NOON

The Christian faith is of so complicated a nature, that unless we give up ourselves entirely to its disciplines, we cannot steadfastly adhere to any of its precepts. All virtues are closely bound together; and break but one link of the golden chain, you spoil the whole contexture. As vices are often made necessary supports to each other; so virtues do mutually strengthen and assist virtues.

Thus temperance and chastity, fortitude and truth, humility and patience, divine charity and charity toward others; all virtues, of what denomination whatsoever, reciprocally cherish and invigorate one another.

MORNING

Philosophy and morality are not sufficient to restrain us from those sins to which our constitution of body, circumstances of life, or evil custom strongly dispose us. Nature and appetite will be too strong, unless we are determined by a law within ourselves.

Philosophy and morality may teach us caution, and check our vicious inclinations in public, but will never carry us to an inward and universal purity. This is only to be effected by the power of our faith, which directs us to a serious supplication to God in fervent prayer, upon which we shall feel a disengagement from the impressions sensual objects may make upon our minds, and an inward strength of disposition to resist them.

Those who have felt upon frequent supplication to God in prayer a freedom from ill impressions that formerly subdued them, an inward love of virtue and true goodness, and an easiness and delight in holiness, and who have languished when it has abated, have had as real a perception of an inward strength in their minds, rising and falling according to devotion in prayer, as they have perceived strength in their bodies increasing or decreasing according to the intake or decrease of nourishment.

EVENING

Our minds are naturally so corrupted and all the powers thereof so weakened that we cannot possibly aspire vigorously toward God or have any clear perception of spiritual things without his assistance. Nothing less than the same almighty power that raised Jesus Christ from the dead can raise our souls from the death of sin to a life of holiness.

To know God experientially is altogether supernatural and that which we can only attain to by the merits and intercession of Jesus Christ. By virtue of what he has done and suffered and is now doing in heaven for us, we obtain the Holy Spirit, who is the best instructor, the most powerful teacher we can possibly have, without whose agency all other means of grace would be ineffectual. How evidently does the Holy Spirit concur with the means of grace!

And how certainly does he assist and strengthen the soul, if it be but sincere and hearty in its endeavors to avoid any evil or perform any good! To have a good desire, a fervent aspiration toward God, shall not pass unregarded.

I have found, by long experience, that it is of great benefit to enter into solemn communion with God against a particular sin; but I would have this fellowship never shorter than from morning till night and from night till morning, so that the impression of such communion may be always fresh and lively. Glory be to you, O Lord!

EVENING

I give God the praise for any well-spent day. But I am yet unsatisfied, because I do not enjoy enough of God. I apprehend myself at too great a distance from him; I would have my soul more closely united to him by faith and love. I can appeal to his omniscience, that I would love him above all things. He that made me knows my desires, my expectations.

My joys all center in him, and it is he himself that I desire; it is his favor, it is his acceptance, the communications of his grace, that I earnestly wish for more than anything in the world; and I have no relish or delight in anything when under apprehensions of his displeasure.

I rejoice in my relationship to him, that he is my Father, my Lord, my God. I rejoice that he has power over me, and I desire to live in subjection to him; that he condescends to punish me when I transgress his laws, as a father chastens the son whom he loves. I thank him that he has brought me thus far; and I will beware of despairing of his mercy for the time which is yet to come, but will give God the glory of his free grace.

MORNING

It is too common with me, upon receiving any light or new supply of grace, to think that now I have arrived and may say, "Soul, take it easy," by which means I think of not going any further; or else I fall into a dejection of spirit upon a groundless fear that I shall soon lose what I have gained, and in a little time be never the better for it.

Both of these are sins. The first proceeds from immoderate love of present ease and spiritual sloth; the other from want of faith in the all-sufficiency of my Savior.

We must never take up our rest on this side of heaven, nor think we have enough of God till we are perfectly renewed and sanctified in body, soul, and spirit; till we are admitted into that blessed region of pure and happy spirits, where we shall enjoy the beatific vision according to the measure of our capacities!

Nor must we, out of a pretended humility, because we are unworthy of the least mercy, dare to dispute or question the sufficiency of the merits of Jesus Christ. It is impossible for God incarnate to undertake more than he is able to perform.

MORNING

Though we are all born to trouble, yet I believe there is scarcely a person to be found upon earth but, take the whole course of that one's life, has more mercies than afflictions, and more pleasure than pain. I am sure it has been so in my case. I have many years suffered much pain and great bodily infirmities, but I have likewise enjoyed great intervals of rest and ease.

And those very sufferings have, by the blessing of God, been of excellent use, and proved the most proper means of reclaiming me from a vain and sinful lifestyle, insomuch that I cannot say, I would have been better without this affliction, disease, loss, want, contempt, or reproach.

All my sufferings, by the admirable management of omnipotent goodness, have concurred to promote my spiritual and eternal good. And if I have not reaped that advantage by them which I might have, it is merely owing to the perverseness of my own will, frequent lapses into present things, or unfaithfulness to the Spirit of God, who, notwithstanding all my misleadings, all the careless oppositions I have made, has never completely abandoned me. Glory be to you, O Lord!

PEACE LIKE A RIVER

Help me, O Lord, to make true use of all disappointments and calamities in this life, in such a way that they may unite my heart more closely with you.

Cause them to separate my affections from worldly things and inspire my soul with more vigor in the pursuit of true happiness.

Until this temper of mind be attained, I can never

enjoy any settled peace, much less a calm serenity.

You only, O God, can satisfy my immortal soul and bestow those spiritual pleasures that alone are proper to its nature.

Grant me grace to stay and center my soul in you; to confine its desires, hopes, and expectations of happiness to you alone; calmly to attend to the seasons of your providence and to have a firm, habitual resignation to your will.

Enable me to love you, my God, with all my heart, with all my mind, with all my strength; so to love you as to desire you; so to desire you as to be uneasy without you, without your favor, without some such resemblance to you as my nature in this imperfect state can bear. Amen.

PRAY IN ALL THINGS

I thank you, O Lord, because never once in my life have I been unheard in what I feared, when I have approached you in a full sense of my own impotence of mind, with humility and sincerity to implore your divine assistance.

I set my seal that you are true, since I have ever found you to be so.

Forbid that I should venture upon any business without first begging your direction and assistance.

Set a check upon my mind when I would do anything that I know to be unlawful or dubious, and encourage me with hope of success in my lawful undertakings. Amen.

Bibliography

Cairns, Earle. *Christianity Through the Centuries.* Grand Rapids, Mich.: Zondervan, 1954.

Clarke, Adam. *Memoirs of the Wesley Family.* New York: Lane and Tippett, 1848.

Dallimore, Arnold. *Susanna Wesley: The Mother of John and Charles Wesley.* Grand Rapids, Mich.: Baker, 1993.

Doughty, W. L. *The Prayers of Susanna Wesley.* New York: The Philosophical Library, 1956.

Edwards, Maldwyn. *Family Circle.* Epworth, London: n.p., 1949.

Kirk, John. *The Mother of the Wesleys.* Jarrold, London: n.p., 1868.

Kline, Donald. *Susanna Wesley: God's Catalyst for Revival.* Lima, Oh.: The C.S.S. Publishing Co., 1980.

Wesley, John. *The Works of John Wesley.* Grand Rapids, Mich.: Zondervan, 14 vols., n.d.

Wesley, John, and Charles Wesley. *Songs and Sermons.* London: Fount Paperbacks, 1996.

Acknowledgments

Many people made this book possible. First, I wish to thank the Lord Jesus Christ for allowing me to write about such a godly woman.

Secondly, I want to especially thank my editor, Steve Laube, and Bethany House Publishers for believing in me and giving me the opportunity to write for them. I also greatly appreciate the input my writing critique group gave me on this manuscript.

Thirdly, I want to thank my husband, Mike, and my three beautiful children, Jessica, Moriah, and Jeremiah for all their love and support. I also want to acknowledge and thank my grandmother, Jennie Rose, who died while I was writing this book. She was a mother to me.

Finally, I want to thank Mindy for taking such good care of my children. I could not have done my work without her love and support.